A New Leaf
1

ALSO BY JIM GOLD

BOOKS

Songs and Stories for Open Ears

Handfuls of Air: A Book of Modern Folk Tales

Mad Shoes: The Adventures of Sylvan Woods:
From Bronx Violinist to Bulgarian Folk Dancer

Crusader Tours and Other Stories

RECORDINGS

World of Guitar
American Folk Ballads

A New Leaf

1

Adventures in the Creative Life

❧

Jim Gold

FCP

Full Court Press
Englewood Cliffs, New Jersey

First Edition

Copyright © 2001 by Jim Gold

Published in the United States of America
by Full Court Press, 601 Palisade Avenue,
Englewood Cliffs, NJ 07632
fullcourtpress.com

ISBN 978-0-9709477-1-0
Library of Congress Control Number: 2020904310

Editing and book design by Barry Sheinkopf

Table of Contents

❧

January–March 1994

April–June 1994

July–September 1994

January-March 1994

WRITING

Voice of My Future

Even though it earns no money, writing is the most important thing I do,

It uncovers higher ground. The sounds of language passing through my mind make me feel great! Gifts rain down when I write.

Writing clarifies meaning and purpose.

It is a calling.

Am I afraid to face it? Wasn't Moses afraid to face *his* calling, afraid of the responsibility and burdens of leadership? Finally, he accepted his destiny and talent, and followed his path.

I am ready to follow mine.

Rise each morning. Write an hour! Create the most important hour of the day.

This morning's voice sounds strange, foreign, wild, yet full of discipline—a cry from the wilderness, a powerful Hibernian wind gusting from arctic heights, blowing away old forms and creating a clearing for the new.

Where will writing lead?

I do not know. But I will follow its voice into my future.

Keep the Pages Flowing!

Keep the pages flowing. Do not stop! I want to write one hour a day. In the process, I want to come up with something of value, and win people's admiration. A little worship from animals wouldn't hurt either—they have souls, even though they can't pay mortgages.

I feel vulnerable whenever I write. I have no idea where my words come from. They seem magical, a gift from above. When I write, ego disappears; my hands become instruments.

No one knows how a word is created. I wrote them yesterday, but will I write them again today?

Every morning I stand at the edge of a cliff, peering through my computer screen into a new abyss.

I jump. . .and hope I can fly.

Pure Flow

I see the mountains of Ararat melting into the sands of the Negev, the peaks of Mount Sinai trembling and bending towards the Balkan rivers. Can these visions be untrue, or should I dance for joy at my release?

I am grinding along the bottom, writing anything I can to fill my daily quota. I practice dexter movement: a thousand fingers fly across the pages as they march to Egyptian pyramids behind a Balkan drum with a Slavic beat. I torture myself by checking the clock. Yet torture is part of the daily quota game. All this without affirmative action.

Can I fill it? Is anyone out there listening, or is this journal too inward? Ha! My confidence is slipping. Otherwise, why ask such a question?

Fishing for the word, phrase, tadpole, or stirrup bender, I'm aiming for pure flow. But will pure flow hold a reader? Is it interesting? Those questions can only be answered later—and by someone else. I cannot concern myself with them. But I do. Will I be loved or embarrassed when this verbal flow is read in public? Will I want to hide if a reader falls asleep?

But just because my audience *may* fall asleep or I *may* get embarrassed does not mean I'm wrong. In spite of human weaknesses my writing is good. Perhaps people will read it in the future.

But suppose, through lack of confidence, I over-edit, discarding jewels, diamonds, gold, and priceless metals? What a crime that would be. Future headlines: *Writer throws jewels into the sea believing they are stones.*

Pure flow in itself is a worthy goal. It is a stranger knocking at my door. Though his face is unclear he nevertheless will be my guest.

Four Pages a Day

My back hurts. I'm drained. Can I write when my back hurts?

Can I write, then throw away my pages?

I'm trying, oh, Lord, I'm trying! Squeezing, pushing, limping, grimacing, pounding the keyboard, sweating to write my four pages and thus squeeze out the hour creating my freedom.

Freedom from what?

Freedom from my obligation to write four pages.

Freedom is my burden. Only a magnificent unobstructed flow of verbiage can set me free.

I'm racing through my vocabulary powerhouse. Gray skies lower outside my window; umbrella people pass my house, huddled in scrunched-up postures, fighting wind, cold, rain, and sleet. They're going to work. I'm home at my computer, trying to create something of value for I don't know whom and I don't know what. It's an endless quest. I could put in hours every day for forty centuries, and still there'll be no end to commitment. Tied to the Promethean rock, pushing Sisyphean rock up a hill for no political cause, ontological rationale, or higher purpose. Where is the sanctified road I can walk upon? Vanished. I pour and pour, hoping to reach the four-page quota.

Perhaps I'm developing a skill, a looseness, a writing fluidity that will someday do me good. But when? And what kind of good? Am I doomed to write in circles for the rest of my life?

Let me look into this.

Is writing in circles so bad? After all, the sun moves in circles; so does the earth; so does the entire solar system. If it's good enough for them, why shouldn't it be good enough for me? Perhaps going in circles is the natural way, the best way. Going in circles may be a talent I never recognized.

For thousands of years mankind has asked, What is the goal of life, its purpose and meaning? Why write, pray, or hope? What about love? I'd love to have readers poring over my words, telling me what significance, meaning, and lofty purpose my work has had on their lives; I want their respect, love, and admiration. But how long would that satisfy me? Probably five minutes. Maybe more, but not much. Would it inspire me to keep writing? I doubt it. It's nice to be loved, respected, and admired, but sadly, not enough to make me write. The writing process has its own magnificence: It's a subtle brand of torture. Maybe I like to punish, afflict, and torture myself. Whipping myself brings blood to my beaten cerebellum. A rush of hot blood fills my brain when I write, flooding my mind and brimming over onto the pages. My suffering gains importance. It pushes me up the spiritual ladder, which is a reward in itself.

Next to this, the love and admiration I might receive from my audience pales in significance. Why would I want love from my audience when I can have my own orgasms writing? Why should I torture myself for their kudos when I can torture myself alone and receive the same benefits? Sick, you say, sick. Solipsism at its worst. You're right. I am an ego-driven maniac, uncaring about others, totally self-involved and considering only the glories, benefits, and ecstasies of my own needs.

Although I follow the Ten Commandments, I really don't care that much about them. Following them doesn't lead to ecstasy.

I am creating The Book of Me, Me, Me. Isn't that immoral, indecent, and selfish? How can I, in good conscience, leave the world to its own miserable devices, forget about the suffering of others, and concentrate only on my own suffering? What about helping others? What about the Golden Rule?

What will Mother say? I, I, I, Me, Me, Me: Is this art? Am I drifting further into myself, and ultimately into insanity? If this is insane, it's not unpleasant. In fact, it borders on glorious. I would love to retreat from the world. Wouldn't I have a safer, happier life just living alone? What could be more entertaining than my own mind?

Perhaps I should give up the idea of this journal being literature, and rather think of it as my survival kit for functioning in the world. Perhaps I should give up the whole idea of "writing literature." What is writing literature, anyway? Henry Miller didn't write literature. He hated literature. Too phony, too pretentious. Rather, just pour out the real stuff, the trials and miseries that make up the suffering of the human condition.

It feels like I'll be writing this journal for the rest of my life. It is so simple, so easy, so natural. The words flow out. No preconceived notions, no plans, no outline or plot to follow. I write whatever I like in whatever order I like. Any crazy thing that comes to mind gets written down. It may interest no one but me, and it may not even interest me. But it serves the wonderful purpose of self-liberation. It is my daily psychoanalysis, my daily adventure into the unknown, the unexplored realm of my self.

It feels like the amount of writing I can do is endless. I can go on and on. Most of it may be drivel, but it is my drivel.

I'm so happy I've discovered this.

And my back feels so much better!

On Finding My Character and Plot

I look at the writings of the last days and I think: Could I have written that awful stuff? Is my judgement completely off? I thought I was on my way to a new writing style, lofty ideas poetically expressed, dynamic metaphors spread in genius fashion across my pages. I am reaching my peak, becoming the Cervantes of modern literature, the James Joyce of word play and innovation. Soon recognition will come, and I will be loved and respected by the critics.

But after reading what I've written, I have to reassess. It hurts. Deception always does.

Still, maybe I'm wrong and just being hard on myself; I'm too close to my writing. My job is to keep on writing, not to judge it. Leave that to others. Their views are not definitive either, but they do give me ideas, directions, and thoughts, or, as a contrarian, something new to say "no" to. A good "no" is like a good shit—it relieves me until the next meal.

Another thing is this idea of plot. I can't seem to write a plot or even think of one. When I do, it dies stillborn. Yet the style of writing I'm doing now—the free-form, stream-of- consciousness style—flows easily and effortlessly from my fingers. Something that comes that easy must have truth in it. Perhaps I'm on to something but don't realize it yet. I'm simply sitting down at the computer and speaking into it—like talking to a friend who'll listen to and accept anything I say.

Will this give me a plot? Or shall I ramble through pages of journal, ever satisfying myself but never writing something worth publishing?

Ah, publication! Reaching my *audience*! Again how I love to be read and appreciated. It tells me I am good, right, and of value. Aye, there's the key. I want to be valued. I want to be worthy of living under God's sky. Who will tell me I am valuable? How can I depend on publication, acceptance, and good reviews to tell me? That will be a worthiness based on past work. Who will tell me I am worthy *today*? I know it should be me, but I'm running out of gas.

The only thing I have to go by is the ease of writing this journal. I love it! Does that make it worthy? Or must it be socially useful, too? Must others appreciate me before my worthiness can be complete?

Why do I rebel against writing a plot? Is it claustrophobia?

Maybe the "I" in my journal is the subject for my plot. The main character is me; the plot is the day-to-day adventures of "me." Readers won't know the "me" I write about. They'll see themselves or another me. What and who is the real me, anyway? Damned if I know. This me that I write about is probably a fiction. Once I wake up in a few weeks or years, I'll read my writing and feel as if someone else wrote it. I'll be living in another dream then.

The Grand Moment

Ah, it is so *freeing* to let words sing and fly helter- skelter across these pages. The wonder of writing them makes my effort worthwhile.

As I sail through the miracle of piling words upon these pages, I thank the forces above for the gift of language. The snow is falling. My day will be quiet, meditative, and pensive, and I am thankful for that. I am thankful for the yesterday morning of exquisite creation, where I did the best I could.

Once in a great while, a grand moment occurs when you break down crying over the beauty of the world, when you realize you are being guided by a Higher Hand. I had such a moment yesterday. Within it lay the essence of all I want. Impossible to describe. I fell to my knees, thankful for the most beautiful gift in the world, the gift of guidance and vision.

Freedom

Freedom is a dangerous thing, especially in my hands. But I can't think of better hands to put it in.

I'm moving upward. Dreams of publication and recognition have disappeared. The weights have fallen off. I'm onto another track, heading in another direction. Free at last!

I'm bathed in the *process itself.* The glory of *it!* Yes, yes, give me my bath of gold!

I'm afraid success will ruin me and I'll never write again. That *would* be a tragedy.

But the suffering may be good for me. God makes me suffer so I can get some work done and, in the process, rise from my surroundings to have a brief transcendental luncheon with Him.

So what else is new? I'm writing comprehensible sentences. What's the matter with me? Is this psychoanalysis? Art? Maudlin, self-absorbed ego chatter? Or am I on my way to a pureer art form, a better means of expression? In other words, will my future pages sing? Will they be read? Will I be loved for the wonderful things I am doing, recognized for the unearthly genius that, deep down, I am?

Dare I describe such grandiose hopes and wishes? But in this "truth" journal I must write whatever comes into my head. All words must be totally uncensored and unedited on the first draft. That's my writing style. I lead a first-draft life. I hate editing. The adventure of flying through a first draft, with all the brilliant, illuminating, and miserable discoveries in it, are the reason I write. Why else waste time sitting and ruminating at the computer? Writing is my personal exercise in self- discovery.

I picture myself turning out volume after volume of *New Leaves* with not a glimmer of publication in sight. I cannot imagine anyone will ever read my writing. Can I write that way? Don't I entertain, deep in my heart, the hope that some day I will be discovered? Even post-humously? I can picture it: A researcher goes through my house, finds my personal belongings and, lo and behold, he discovers my writing! He is amazed, mesmerized. What genius! he exclaims. I have found an unknown treasure. This incredible literary work must be published at all costs. I soon become world famous, and all the barings of my heart and soul go public. That is one of my fantasies. That means *I am secretly writing for an audience.*

Who is my audience? I don't know. But that's not as important as the fact that I am writing for one. Would I write if I believed no one would ever read my work? Could I communicate with nobody forever? Could such an empty vision sustain me?

If I am writing for an audience in the quiet of my room, it means I am still performing. Yes my writing is a private performance, just as my guitar concerts are public performances. In the closet of my mind, I am still a performer.

Who am I performing for?

God?

An audience?

Both?

Both sound right.

Audiences come in all forms: customers, wives, children, people I speak to on the street. . . .

What about the idea of writing as a good-in-itself?

Is it a good-in-itself?

In order to be good-in-itself, it must have transcendental value.

Does it?

The answer is a paradox! My writing is *both* transcendental and au-dience driven; it is a good-in-itself as it reaches out to an imaginary audience.

The Entrepreneurial Life

I'm discouraged this morning.

Discouraged?

Why?

Just because poor registration forced me to cancel a weekend, just because my dance classes are small and winter weather is killing my business? Just because there have been no tour or weekend registrants for the last six weeks and I spent two thousand dollars on a news brochures and mailings, and my business is almost totally dead? Just because I'm running out of money, going into debt, and so miserable? Is that a reason to be discouraged?

Absolutely not, as long as you remain unreasonable.

Irrational, insane, visionary, delusional, are the best qualities to get you through bad times. Any reasonable person would have given up, not weeks or months, but *years* ago.

But I am not unreasonable. I'm too crazy to give up. I'll be pushed into a corner first, whipped, beaten, pulverized, and destroyed, but I'll never give up. I'm too proud to admit or accept defeat. I'd rather die first. And my business is dying. But do I see it that way? No. For me it's a temporary relapse.

What is this quality about me? Why won't I quit and move on to something else? I've been running some of my miserable low-to-no-paying folk dance classes for years, and for some crazy reason I won't give them up. I'll always find an excuse, no matter how ridiculous, to continue.

Am I courageous and indomitable? Am I nuts? Am I having a permanent, long-range temper tantrum? *Never, never, never!* I keep screaming as I kneel on the living room floor and pound it with my fists. Why won't people register? Why won't they call me and send me deposits for all the great events I am running? Why won't they show up in droves for the beautiful folk dance classes, the inspired weekends, the adventurous world tours? Where *are they?*

But if I wait for them to make up their minds, I'll end up doing nothing. So I go about my business, or lack of business, limping along with those few who do show up, living on the edge, worried about money, pounding the table, and kicking the chair. Such is the life of an entrepreneur.

Hero Road

My purpose is to create a flow, not an original work. Let the river run. If a beautiful mermaid appears, or an octopus swims, or a rising sea monster grabs my boat, it does not matter, so long as my creations flow. And each word is my creation, even repeated a thousand times. The world vision rises, and marches, and sags through tantalisms of cataclysmic atrocities, wrenching abnormalities, chilling, distant, cry-screaming abodes located deep in the antipodes, where words sing in gold mine shafts and laser miners stub their toes on gold and silver bars.

Strike out on a new path, the dynamic Hero Road. The customary byways are heavy with blood. Ancient sewers are burning.

Home Is All Directions

I'm hanging by my finger nails—no plot, structure, or form—dangling in mid-air, wondering where my next shelf will be. Is this a way to write? Such free forms leading nowhere and everywhere at the same time?

But what else can I do? This journal is my destiny. I can only follow an inner voice that says, *Go in all directions to find home.*

Why apologize for my style? Why search any further? I am home immediately writing down what comes to mind. What's the difference if my writing is incomprehensible? I'm not publishing for a general market but for the one, two, or more in tune with me. Who can understand *Finnegan's Wake?* Not many. (Not even Joyce.) But so what? Why judge everything based on *comprehension?* Is beauty comprehensible? As soon as you understand it, it disappears. Only the ugly is understandable, because it is so awful you want to understand it to make it go away.

I like writing babble. I like the fact that I can't understand it. It makes reading an adventure. I'm not even sure who's writing it. Is that my voice or a foreign one creeping into my brain through the left ear? Who can say?

Foreign voices can be intriguing and say things I would never think of.

I hate reading my work when I remember it was I who wrote it. I enjoy it only when I've forgotten the author. And even when I remember I am the *author*, I'm not sure who I am, anyway.

Who am I? Beats me. I'm not interested in finding out. If I ever do, I'll start looking for someone else.

Losing interest in who I am frees me. I don't care what I write. Any word, phrase, sentence, or paragraph will do; as long as I keep stringing words across the pages, I am happy. In doing so, I discover vast regions of the unknown.

The known world bores me.

Home is all directions.

LANGUAGES

Returning to Languages

I am returning to conversational Hebrew, Hungarian, Czech, Bulgarian, and Turkish.

Back to pages that flow and sing, sounds of Old English and Middle English, Old Norse and biblical Hebrew, medieval Hungarian and Church Slavonic, medieval Bulgarian and beyond. Weld and fuse these ancient languages with modern Norwegian, Icelandic, Bulgarian, Czech, Hebrew, and Turkish.

How I love language! The sound and music of it ties my lips to the mouths of others.

Our glorious, soul-kissing tongues will meet in Turkish, Hebrew, Norwegian, Bulgarian, Czech, Hungarian, French, Spanish, and Italian.

Tours, languages, adventures in foreign lands: I see horizons expand before me. Speak to a live Bulgarian on native soil or a Hungarian, Czech, Israeli, or whatever—that's a thrill to repeat and repeat!

Dear Language, I am coming! I tour every year to meet you and make love to your lips.

LIFE

Security

What a shock to realize that, for the creative individual, security does not exist—and that all human beings are creative, though much of their daily creation consists in denying their creativity by searching for safety.

Are the dead creative, too? Perhaps, but quietly so.

Security is an illusion.

There is only *the hope* for security, the hope that somewhere in a future paradise it will exist for you. Hope for that drives you on, fuels your daily fare.

Felucca of Perfection

One of the Egyptian mysteries is the remembrance of perfection.

How do you reach perfection? By walking the broken road of *imperfection*.

Witness the name of the Nile river boat *felucca*. I knew it lay hidden somewhere deep in my memory. Had I waited for it to rise correctly spelled from my memory bank, I would have waited hours. I would never have written a thing. Instead, I fished for the sound, misspelled it again and again. Finally, when the time was right, it rose instantaneously and mysteriously from my inner computer. Then it sprung from my mind and jumped on the page. Perfection!

A Sunday Morning Walk Through the Words

Can this existence be serious?

How can anything be serious that dies tomorrow?

Time is an illusion.

I'm giving up my plans. When tomorrow comes, I may not be here to greet it. And "tomorrow" doesn't mean twenty-four hours. It means next year, five years from now, fifty years, centuries, millennia, even millions of years of geological time. Seconds, and millions of years, are only quantitative differences. Qualitatively, time remains an illusion.

How can I break through it? I am disgusted with the movie screen my transient human mind considers to be reality. I have asked too much of the world. It cannot give me what I want. I am looking in the wrong room for permanence and light.

Why pursue these goals, which lead to dis-appointment and emptiness? Can this transient body really be all there is to me? Can those of my friends be all there is to them? Haven't I known them previously in other forms? And if this is so, why worry about money, death, business discouragements, failed tours or weekends, or folk dance class cancellations? What's the worst that can happen? I'll die. That's it. Is that really so bad? Or is living worse? Good questions for a Sunday morning walk through the words.

I May Be Alone, But I Ain't Lonely

I am never going back to the old days. Never, never, never!

The days of slavery are over. I'd rather die alone, stuck in a hollow carved out of a mountain oak, than return to the bending, twisting, cringing, of constant fear and the pain of other-directed slavery. Sure, I may end up standing alone, but at least I can roar my lions's roar of freedom. I may be alone, but I sure ain't lonely.

If I don't satisfy others, they often complain and blame me. Perhaps I am partly to blame because of my limitations as a human being. But these limitations are not going to end even if I'm dissatisfied. Limitations are part of the human condition. Criticism of me is besides the point. I'm going to do what I have to.

So be it.

Joy Is All I Have Left

Why am I so depressed this morning?

Could it be from the collapse of Greenwich Pharmaceuticals? I bought 1,000 shares at 2 ½. It went to 4, then collapsed to 1 . Now it may well go bankrupt. The same thing happened with Martech—collapsed from 8 to near bankruptcy. I bought 2500 at ¾ and it immediately went to 2. Now it's back to 1, and every day I wonder about bankruptcy. My stocks are doing miserably. No one has registered for my tours in the last three weeks. I've had four cancellations. That's mucho money lost. Only three people have registered for the President's Day Weekend. My folk dance classes are diminishing—especially Monday night's. Business is miserable; I'm losing money.

These are all good reasons to be depressed. But they're not good enough for me. I've been through this routine many times before. It's the nature of business, the nature of life. Vicissitudes—how can I take them seriously? They're annoying, but they come and go like a will of the wisp. Can a grown man base his happiness on vicissitudes?

My blues are a habit. If I ride the currents of up and down long enough, eventually I take them seriously; soon I begin believing they are the only reality. Fear of losing money is a reality. Do I believe in this fear? Not really.

I hate to admit it, but I'm happy!

Do I dare believe it? There's no other choice. My old habits have been unveiled, and in the harsh light of introspection they simply fall apart. There's no reason to worry about money unless I've got nothing better to do with my mind. Sure, I could lose all any day now, just as I could lose my life. Every living thing is up for grabs, including me. It's up to God. Whatever He wants.

I asked a person from Ethical Culture if God exists, and she answered, "It's up to you. It's your choice." *My choice?* What power that gave me—and what insecurity. But the whole thing is ridiculous. Of course God exists. He's running my fate and deciding my future. I'll put in my best effort, but nevertheless, I have no control about ultimate things such as death and marketing.

I'm ready for a new habit. Stocks, business, career, money, could all collapse. Let's not take the ephemeral too seriously. I need something everlasting. If I give up depression and choose joy, can I stand it? Can I survive happiness? But I see no other choice. Old Man Depression doesn't fool me anymore. His bite is gone; he's a shadow of his former self, just another guy hanging around the store waiting for a lift home. Sure, I'll give him a hand, why not? But to give him all this power? Forget it. That's over.

The Bible says it's okay to be joyful; so do the Vedas and yogic writings. The only one who really opposed it was my mother, and my teachers in the first and second grades.

Joyful attitude, joyful life: tough challenge. But my old habits have been exposed as frauds. Joy is all I have left.

Land Beyond Recognition

The Land Beyond Recognition is where the saints dwell. God has a residence upstairs. It faces the Park of Eternity and Infinity.

The Land Beyond Recognition is not of this world. How can I enter? One foot here, one foot there: a workable compromise. Dual citizenship. The trick is doing—and thinking—two things at once. Perhaps that's why we have dual organs: two feet, two arms, two eyes, two ears—one for the lower world and one for the upper.

Give Me the Beautiful World. . .

What would Galileo, Newton, Descartes or Kant say? These giants return me to the University of Rochester, University of Aix-en-Provence, University of Chicago, City College of New York, and to my fifth floor walk-up apartment on St. Marks Street in the East Village, where I sat in my stuffed armchair, reading and dreaming about the great philosophies of the world. I loved those beautiful thoughts swirling about my head, making mincemeat of the miserable make-a-living realities I had to face beyond my door. Give me the beautiful world of study. Free me from strain, pain, frustration, and grasping. Who wouldn't want to be free?

A better question is, how can I get such freedom?

My hubris says I should be writing something great created out of the mysterious stew of my dreams, imagination, hopes, fears, and competition with Descartes, Kant, etc. Could I go on without this hubris?

If I give it up, will I have to settle for mediocrity? Will levelness and evenness be the flat, boring road I travel on?

Is mediocrity so bad? It does take the pressure off and levels the playing field. However, I may fall asleep on such a field, and, although sleep is not a bad thing, you cannot capture the moral high ground by sleeping all day.

This all boils down to a problem of direction, which raises its ugly disgusting head almost every day of my life. Why was I born? Where am I going? Why do I have to repeat the same questions over and over again? Why do I keep going round in circles? Am I a metaphor of the human condition? Can an artist live a lifestyle going round in circles, coupled with mediocrity?

It's embarrassing to whine and complain about going in circles, to bore others with constant repetitions. I expect more from myself: originality, new insights, exploration of the unknown; to ride into the stratosphere, grabbing stars and galaxies along the way, and someday to return to earth with a messianic message of immortality and hope that will save the world. Unrealistic? Perhaps. But who cares? That is my dream. After I save the world, people will tell me how worthy I am.

Perhaps this is crazy. But what else should I do with my life? Megalomania is a fine middle name.

No wonder I start off every day disappointed. I've got high standards.

Saving the world is no easy task, especially since every night it slips backwards to zero. All the good work I did yesterday seems as nothing today. I've got to start all over again. This world refuses to be saved.

When I Lose, I Win

Values rule the world in transcendental form. I know my values and what's important to me; I know what I love.

When I do what I believe in, I shine. Power, strength, and happiness radiate from my being. Misery, too. That's part of the struggle. Since I know what I want, it's very important that I do what I want. Thus, pushing and driving myself, eliminating excuses, fitting my body and mind with tough love, make me happy! When I say no to sloth and, instead, get up early in the morning to put in my hour of writing, I feel great! When I run an hour despite the "fact" I "have no time" or "don't feel like it," I end up like an accomplished master of my own fate. Yes, I can achieve things even though I'm feeling miserable, weak, sick, and listless.

Yes, I can run, write, perform, or whatever is important in spite of the sense that every fiber of my being is crying out: Give up!

But when I follow the road of ease, give in to the forces of sloth, I'm like a blown-out, decaying failure, and no hero to myself.

I want to be my own hero. When I fight the dragons of defeat and decay that daily rise up within me, I stand up for my better self. I may go down fighting but I don't give up. Then, even when I lose, I win.

Life as an Asymptote

The asymptotic responsibility of a snow-driven day arrives early and tangentially for me this morning. What a pleasure to live life like an asymptote: always approaching, but never touching. It gives a sense of perspective.

"Blundering Babble!" He Cried

Only the deaf are blind this morning. And why not? Can't you see the barren, empty morning sky sitting pregnant above me? How can this be? Pregnant and barren at the same time? Surely, a paradox, but it needs no explaining. Why introduce an audience where there is none? Paradox and nonsense and irrationality are all my middle names—perhaps last name, too. So, onwards and sidewards we go, marching to the jazzy tune of an 11/16ths drummer pounding out Bulgarian *kopanica* rhythms on a snowbound Fried Day.

White, white, white, the incessant snows are falling. Dancing caterpillars populate my lawn while trees sing in leafless splendor. Can a wasp germinate among such wires? Telephone poles are down, but communications are up. How can that be?

I woke up with a blinding headache. Why? I'll never know why. Perhaps it is because America is falling apart. The political mode impinges on my peace of mind. I heard Dennis Prager on the radio yesterday. A wonder, he.

He said, I have the answer for happiness: it is *gratitude*. Imagine that, gratitude. If you have gratitude, you can be happy. What a novel twist. What about psychotherapy and psychoanalysis, which make you miserable? What about complaining about politics, crime, welfare, health care, racism, affirmative action, infirmative action, Bosnia, on and on, all of which make you unhappy? How can misery and dissatisfaction survive if you have gratitude? The misery industries will crumble if gratitude takes over. They have a vested interest in promoting unhappiness. It's just business, folks. Just let gratitude in, just let in a little happiness, and you'll see a depression and economic destruction rarely witnessed in history. Misery industries will be hit hard. They may end up on the dole, needing government support. Welfare for the health industry. Gratitude? Forget it. If it does come, we'll fight it tooth and nail.

Yet it is true: Gratitude brings happiness. Rich or poor, poss- essions or no possessions, gratitude is a state of mind anyone can possess. Thus, it is within everyone's power to be happy. But it's a struggle. You've got to be a rebel to fight against the prevailing mood. You'll be shot down at every turn. Lots of traps on the gratitude road. Still, it is a wonderful road to follow. What a challenge.

On the other hand, who wants to be grateful anyway? It's much more fun to complain. Complaining often makes my day. I like to hear others complaining, too. Then I can complain about their complaining. Complaints help pass the time while the snow keeps falling. . . like dandruff.

Rambling Through Annoyances

It's Saturday afternoon, not the greatest time to write, especially after having put in a two-hour-and-fifteen-minute run . . . still, the world of words awaits me and I must follow my compulsions, callings, and commitments. Meanwhile the horrible background radio disturbs me, but Bernice won't turn it off. I've closed fifteen doors and it still doesn't shut out the miserable sound. Well, what can you do? Also, a pain in the ass is my Paint Plus computer program. Perhaps we should call it Paint Minus. It runs okay, only for some godforsaken reason it won't print. Ask my fucking printer to print it and all it does is spew out page after unstoppable *presque-blanque* pages with incomprehensible computer scribble on it. What the hell it all means, I don't know.

Sounds like I'm angry this afternoon. Well, I *am* angry, damn angry. It's the Paint program that's jamming my nerves. I can't stand the fact it doesn't work! I hate it, hate, hate, hate it! My artistic creations are stymied in the bud. Plus, I don't really know who can fix it. A vague hope resides in the phone number of the creators and producers of Paint Plus, and if I can find them, I'll ask them about it. If their line isn't busy, and if they still exist as a company, then maybe, just maybe, they can help me. If not, I can't call Wordperfect. First, their line is always busy. Besides, they don't know about Paint Plus. Next in line is Frank Carbone, my computer man and maven. He's a good hope. I like him. He's helpful, and he'll try. Only problem is, he may not know what to do. If he doesn't, I'm really up the creek. I doubt if Ben knows, or even David. If I run out of options and no one knows how to get the fucking thing to print, then I've really got a long-term problem. It could go on for weeks, months, or forever. Well, I'll get started and knock off my options one by one.

I'm also annoyed because this long run has worn me out. My frustration tolerance is very low. The slightest noise or annoyance makes me jump. I'm on edge, and the Paint Plus program mess just makes things worse. This, plus I heard Miki is investing in Mutual Funds that only go up. Her friend is a mutual funds maven and studies them all day with her computer. She's given Miki good advice, and Miki's money keeps growing. Bernice, too—her mutual funds investments keep going up. Makes me mad! Why aren't *my* fucking funds going up? One reason is, I don't have any. That's also a good reason to get mad. Well, actually I have some money, but it's not invested in mutual funds, only in stocks. But those stocks have been going nowhere for years. Well, that's not quite true. Actually, they've been going up and down for years; the result of all that movement is they have gone nowhere. I have as much money now as I did two years ago. Joel is a nice guy and he does a good job of service, but his stock picks either go down or nowhere. Once in awhile something goes up, but it's a rare occasion. So I opened my own low commission account with Fidelity to see if I could do better than Joel. After two years my results are about as bad a his. And yet I keep investing; I keep looking for individual stocks and buying them at what I consider to be good prices and waiting, hoping they'll go up. Something in me just hates to put my money in mutual funds. No zing, no zip. I like to choose the companies; I like to feel glorious and super smart when my picks go up, and, although I hate feeling miserable and super stupid when my picks go down, I realize you can't get the ups without the downs. If I buy Mutual Funds, whether they go up or down, I'm so far removed, so insulated from the stock picks and investment decisions, that I won't feel much of an up or down. At least that's where I am now.

But a compromise is in the making. I'll buy a few mutual funds, put say 10 to 20 percent of my assets in mutual funds—see how they make out.

Maybe I can learn to love mutual funds if I buy them and they keep going up.

Another thing that's starting to annoy me is these creepy people who write me about tours. Who the fuck are they, anyway? I know they're answering the ad I put in International Travel News, or perhaps the one in the Paramus Adult Education Bulletin, or a public relations release I don't know about. They've been responding for about a month, and I've been sending them lots of information with lots of my own personal hopes attached. Well, I haven't heard diddledeesquat from any of them. For all I know they're either dead or dying, or have decided to take two-year side trips to the moon. Where the hell are you, fucking people! Sign up, goddammit! Send me your fucking money, send me some checks, send me some deposits, send me *any-thing*. . .no, not anything, only money. Hey, it's miserable and lonely out here just getting advertisements and junk mail with every mail delivery. Where are the fucking people?

Well, fuck 'em all, that's what I say. I'll send them my tour info with *no hopes* attached.

Unfortunately, I still pop them on my mailing list, even though I may never hear from them again in this life. I'm sure they'll be the first to register for my Next Life Tours when it sponsors small intimate group tours to the after life. Cheap, too.

I'm getting sick of their complaining and their snide remarks and their backward commentaries on my marvelous tours. It's true, of course, that they're not *really* complaining. I know that because I don't hear anything from them. Truth is, I don't know what they're doing, what they're thinking, or even if they're thinking at all. Maybe they don't exist; maybe they're phantoms who send me phantom mail with phantom addresses. Who knows? What a stupid frustrating business. Best thing to do, best way to handle it, is to give up.

Now I feel much better.

It's like going to heaven after a tough day on Earth. Why worry? Me, worry? What, *me* worry? Worry, me?

Relax. Have a Coke. Sip some wine, or beer, or purple marmalade soda. Look out over the vast infinity of heaven and give thanks that you're not a hotel operator.

Do It!

I'd like to learn a new skill. But to what purpose? Leaning Hebrew is deepening an old skill. Does that count?

I'd like to add an hour of reading fiction to my schedule. The Tales of Hajji Baba, a 19th-century novel by Morier, an English diplomat to Persia, gave me the idea. It takes place mostly in Isfahan.

I feel so worthy when I perform these pearly activities.

I know what's good for me. I just have to do it.

Fifteen-Year Temper Tantrum

Could all this be the result of a fifteen-year temper tantrum? Is it possible things could move is such long, slow, apparently interminable cycles? The damn problems seem to last forever. Work, work, work, and/or wait, wait, wait, for years and years. Still nothing happens. How can it take so long? Maybe we're on the wrong track? But we keep sticking around, hanging it out, fighting, arguing, sulking, refusing to compromise, locking horns. But it's thawing now. Why, I'll never know. Must be timing. But so long, fifteen years. Is it possible? So long? Must be. There is no other explanation. Look what happened with my guitar playing. That waiting period took over thirty years. Now I'm back to my original guitar, my original love of music. I've stripped away the audience; I'm going real slow and loving it. "Alhambra" is easy at last. It only took thirty years of daily practicing, pounding out that tremolo day after day, changing from high speed to low speed to medium speed to no speed, all in the hope of playing like Segovia before an adoring audience. I knew during all those years my desire to play like Segovia was ridiculous, untrue to myself, unhealthy, burdensome, bothersome, annoying, and sick beyond belief. But knowing it didn't stop me from doing it. Somehow I had to live through the miserable process of personal transformation. Finally, one day, my old skin just fell off and was forgotten. It took thirty years.

If thirty years worked for the guitar, why not a fifteen- year temper tantrum?

That's what my intuition tells me. I know my intuition is right even when my intellect is wrong.

I've had several physical breakthroughs in the last few days. I ran two and a quarter hours on Saturday. Is this the post- fifty-six new beginning? Am I preparing for the next twenty- eight-year cycle?

I also did eighty sit-ups yesterday. Usually I do forty or fifty in counts of two. Eighty! And no pain! I couldn't believe it. I felt I could go on. But it scared me, so I stopped. Today, I thought I'd do fifteen or twenty "recovery" sit-ups. Instead, I easily did sixty, and again with no pain.

What is happening here? Am I moving to a new level?

If I am, what about my writing, push-ups, squats, and music? I did the scorpion yoga pose I've been doing for years.

But suddenly, it got better! I held a longer balanced position on a one-legged squat: That had improved, too. Improvements don't come incrementally, but in blasts of sudden growth. You work and work for months, even years. Nothing seems to happen.

Then suddenly, one day, for no apparent reason, everything bursts into blossom.

You move effortlessly upwards to the next level.

Leading a First-Draft Life

Yesterday my Hewlett Packard ink jet printer died. I replaced it with a Citizen Prolaser jet printer. This morning I noticed it has a high hum. Had I paid $700 for a high hum? Do printers hum? I don't remember. Perhaps I'll get used to it. Meanwhile, it's a pain in the ass.

I'm discouraged, nervous, and bordering on panic this morning. Business feels like it's falling apart. Two months ago I was roaring along with high hopes for tours, weekends, classes, and lots of money. Now I've back-slid into high expenses and low income. Sure, the miserable weather and all the snows have helped destroy things.

Last night we had the Hameed African Dancers. Juanita Hameed is a fantastic teacher and dancer. But the response of my miserable folk dancers was: Only four paying people showed up. This, plus six nonpayers, gave me a total of ten. Thus I immediately lost mucho money. Added to the new printer costs, today became a very expensive day. There must be a lesson in this somewhere. I'm going around in economic circles. Money, money, money—all I think about is money and how I don't have it. I keep spending it, too. An endless sieve. Where are the people? Why don't they send me more money? Why don't they register for tours, weekends, and dance classes?

Then it struck me, as I moped around the dance floor last night, waiting for my nondancers and nonpaying participants to show up: Suppose my financial problem was due to me?

What a radical idea. I'd always thought the problem was everybody else. That's the answer I've been giving most of my business life. But truth is, when I have more money, I spend more money. When money rolls in, I make sure the money rolls out by buying more stocks, more equipment, more anything. The only thing that seems to dampen my spending enthusiasm is poverty.

Complaining

Complaining is wonderful. It is a balm in the ointment of misery. Thank you, O Great One, for giving me the power; for a few moments I am, not happy, but at least not unhappy. One thing about complaining, though—don't try it too much with friends. Most of them won't listen long. I can't blame them. It gets boring. Too personal. That's why writing is so great. You can complain on and on and, in the process, keep all your friends. They will enjoy you because you'll be more upbeat and positive: All your negativity has been strewn across the pages. You're released fresh and pure into the world.

Questions

I ask questions. I start the day with one; after lunch, I have another; after supper, still more. By bedtime I am tired of them. I ask myself, Why do I have so many?

But that itself is a question.

There must be some good in asking them. If not, why would I?

The Five-Minute Approach to Death and Rest

Dry day. Nothing in my head.

I need a rest day.

But I hate rest days, hate giving up the rhythm of work that becomes a hypnotic drug.

Soon I worship my work schedule rather than the energy that gave it birth. By then my creative cycle has run out. I'm preparing to die and be buried. . . and be reborn. Rest days are my death throes, because rest and death are sisters.

Celebration

Thank God the tour to Budapest and Prague over. I snapped yesterday and am looking forward to snapping some more. I can't wait for the time when I won't see anyone. Alone, alone, how wonderful that will be!

I don't mind the people. Rather, it's the constant pressure of "being on." It's okay for awhile, but I've had enough—I need a break. I want to celebrate. This tour was near perfect. Perfection raises the question: Where do I go from here? The answer is: *nowhere*. Perfection is going nowhere and being everywhere at once. All you can do is bathe in its glory.

Traveling the Route of Inner Vision

As Joseph Campbell says, it is difficult for the hero to reenter the world, even more difficult than leaving it. By leaving it, the hero has listened to and followed his inner voice; he has gone to the mountain top, found his vision, developed it. Now comes the return. He is ready to bring his vision back into the world. But the world does not want it. It lacks this vision. That is what the hero sensed and why he left the world in the first place.

What to do?

He can say, "Fuck you all!" and return to his mountain cave.

Or he can say, "I've got a skill. I can help others. What do they want? I'll find out and give it to them." This is the commercial route. Although it may lead to public success, it can also lead to inner deadness and an ultimate denial of his vision. Finally, he can look for the few, the very few who appreciate his vision, give it to them, and slowly, painfully, patiently develop his own following. This route, although often attended by little public acclaim or success (though these *may* come), ensures the faithfulness of his road. It leads to inner peace and satisfaction.

The last road is mine. I've tried the fuck-'em-all approach. It doesn't work for me. I can't drop the public and live forever in my cave—although I often think I want to.

But whenever I've tried it, after a few days I get frustrated and want to return to the fight. If I only retreat and withdraw, my fighting spirit starts to die. I must fight in the world for my vision, struggle to bring it to others, contend for registrations and sales. This, although I often hate it, is my nature.

I can't follow the commercial route either. Personally, I have nothing against it, but it is *not* my nature. As soon as I ask, "What do *they* want?" I lose interest. The commercial route does not work for me. I am too stubborn.

Thus I must travel the "compromise" route, the route of inner vision and outer sales. Joseph Campbell says you do not have a complete adventure unless you return to the world. Life fluctuates between the cave and the world. This approach, he says, leads to inner peace. Perhaps.

Crawling on All Fours Here on Earth

Am I ready to renounce my desires for tour, folk dance, weekend, and financial success?

I would love to do so, to live in peace. Withdrawal is such a fine word. This morning I especially love it.

Why?

I'm scattered, my mental energies pulled in so many directions. Focus and concentration bring me peace. By whittling down my interests to just a few, I think I can achieve it.

But, alas, this is only a pipe dream.

I shall never achieve peace.

I am doomed to struggle in contradiction all my life, to live in total paradox and suffer unending ups and downs.

So be it. Failure, successes, wondrous sales, sickness, broken bones, muscle growth, all the bumps in the traveler's life, are mine, since I am so helplessly mortal. I can touch God with a fingernail once in awhile, but most of the time I'm crawling on all fours here on Earth.

The Voice Straight from Hell

The most important thing in art and life is to follow your inner voice. Be true to that tiny squeak of truth emanating from deep within the bowels of your being.

This is the voice of growth, of knowledge beyond the static; it's the mystic vision, the ineffable, the unknown, the higher powers within. To deny it is to deny aspects of your highest nature.

Yet catering to its demands often leads across the line of reason, tradition, and cultural acceptance into a strange alien land of lan-guishing forms, giant, black-domed mountains, unfordable gulfs, iron trees laced with concrete gates, and monsters of unimaginable ferocity.

Are there more monsters in the inner world than the outer? Is the latter a reflection of the former? Do we create both from a tiny bubble in the brain?

We do.

This bubble is leading me into the land of the unknown.

I need courage. Beyond that, I have little choice.

A voice within is forcing me to follow, telling me it is unfair, nay, a tragedy, to leave this road unexplored, that unseen treasures await me, that I would be blowing a fantastic opportunity not to take it. It may be a rough road, but not embarking would be rougher.

The road of the unknown is a wicked path full of barbed wire, bombs, barbs, and the incomprehensible. It's the passion road. White jolts of irrationality come dressed in raw emotions and new verbal creations.

Ordinary English cannot describe the mystic eruptions emanating from the black boiling bubble within. Only cacophonous word creations come close. I can taste them rising, boiled and impure, from the inner cesspool of my being.

They ascend through stomach, pancreas, lungs, and trachea, lodging for a moment in my throat just below the uvula before bursting past tongue and tooth, blasting lips apart and pouring their distended, bloated bodies onto my pages.

What can I do? I feel helpless before the onslaught. Barriers fall. The rush and challenge of new forms hurtles past the gates, unstoppable in fury and freshness.

Cosmic Purpose

Childish voices still scream at me from the back door of my mind. They are one of many voices I heard as a child. I hear too many voices.

Would deafness be an improvement? One voice at a time would be better. But who knows from better?

I take what comes, and what comes is usually an unfathomable, indecipherable, tangled, mixed-up mess. Journal writing clears up the mess. I dump my shopping bag on the table and put all the new purchases neatly in the closet.

In many respects my mind is like Pathmark. Every day, I push my cart down the aisle, choosing goods from one shelf or another. Then I pay at the check-out counter.

My journal is my personal check-out counter.

All my ideas are added up, printed out on a sales slip column, and handed to me. I bag my stuff, push my cart through the door, and head home.

This morning I read an article in *Forbes* about an executive, educator, and writer who moved to the Virgin Islands and works there permanently.

Since he moved to Paradise he has increased his work time, forging ahead uninterrupted for five hours every morning. Then he goes sailing or swimming.

The article made me jealous. I thought about moving. How nice to live in an island paradise far from the miseries of this world. Then I realized I envied the man's ability to work creatively for five straight hours. *That's* what I wanted. If I could do it, I would be living in paradise.

The point is, working five straight uninterrupted creative hours is well within my grasp. I don't have to move or change location. But I do have to *change my mind set*. I have to be able to focus and disengage my mind from the many trivial and annoying "necessities" plaguing my life. Many of these so- called necessities are business related; most have to do with money. Yet with proper organization I could do both: put in my five-hour mornings of creative work and run my business.

Why don't I? First I must *give myself permission to devote mornings to creative work*. That means six or seven a.m. to noon.

MONEY AND ITS BRETHREN

Reading the Future: The Art of Prediction

All my stocks are going up. Up, up, up.

I'm an excellent stock picker. Only problem is, I sold them long ago. Yes, they were my stocks, but are no longer my stocks. I bought the right companies, but I sold too early. That's because I couldn't read the future.

In order to succeed in the stock market I must be able to read the future. How do I predict it? By visualizing trends. And by using my imagination.

Love of Worry

I had Chinese food last night.

When I opened my fortune cookie, the paper inside read, "You will enjoy good health; that is your form of wealth."

I like that. Perhaps it explains why I'm not making any money in the market.

It might also explain why I'm not rich. I was not meant to be rich. But my worries have always been about money, not about my health. Maybe if I stopped worrying about money, I would worry about my health instead. I like to worry.

Worry must be good for me. Maybe it energizes me, protects me from something worse. Or maybe it's just a bad habit. There must be other benefits to worry. It is often, for example, my warning signal: Something dangerous is coming up. Be careful. I should learn to *love my worry*—and *use it* to energize myself. Why worry? The answer is: why not? Just because it doesn't *feel* good doesn't mean it isn't good. It's just part of living—like having a leg. Negative forces can be helpful. Denying them, shutting them out, may diminish my own force. Therefore, face the devil and use him.

How do you turn worry into starlight, darkness into a beam of light?

PERFORMANCE

Stage Fright

My lower back is grinding out a new tune this morning. It's a return to the old back ache. Why? A booking this morning. I'm doing a school program. I haven't done one for a year, and all the old performing fears have returned. Even though there'll only be fifty middle-school kids in the audience, I've been worried about this show for a month.

Has nothing changed? I'm just as nervous as always. Perhaps it's the nature of my performing. No "perhaps"—it *is*. Nervousness before every new challenge is the only way I know, a habit, I can't do much about. I can go to shrinks, rationalize like crazy, figure out all kinds of reasons why I *shouldn't* be nervous—I'm a good guitarist, I'm charismatic, I sing well, I've got personality, I've done hundreds of shows before, I'm older now and more mature. . .I can go on and on with the explanations and rationalizations, but, truth is, I'm just as anxious as if I'd started yesterday.

That's why I'll just have to accept stage fright as part of the baggage of existence. My performance anxiety never goes away. The only way it will disappear is if I give up performing. But I also get nervous before folk dance classes, weekends, and tours. It can't be "cured." Instead of fighting, denying, or hoping it will go away, I'll begin by dealing with it, by *handling it*.

How? One way of handling it is by writing about it. Aha, I like that. Turn angst into creativity; turn self-torture into the torture of others—namely, my readers. Strangely, my back feels better now.

Make the Supreme Effort

Mihaly Csikszentmihalyi, in his book *Flow: The Psychology of Optimal Experience,* writes: "The best moments usually occur when a person's body or mind is stretched to its limit in a voluntary effort to accomplish something difficult and worthwhile."

What wisdom! Fulfilling my Miracle Schedule does just that. It brings me my best moments; it is tough and worthwhile. Take writing: I'm doing an hour a day. It's difficult and needs my fullest concentration.

Writing stretches my mind to the absolute limit. When I finish my hour, I feel great! I've given my best, made my maximum effort. Others can judge how worthwhile the *product* is, but there's no denying the *worthiness of my effort*. Stretching my mental muscles to their limit creates the optimal moment.

There's also the "first fatigue," which usually comes after thirty of forty minutes. If I push beyond it and break the forty-minute barrier, I explore new ground. During those moments, discoveries and crazy new ideas filter down. I ascend into the unknown.

This is true in running, guitar playing, studying Hebrew, teaching folk dancing, or the other efforts I make. Going that extra mile, running for extra speed, is when I create the runner's high, the exhilaration I feel after two hours, the *I did it!* feeling. Even though my body aches and I limp, crawl, and can hardly walk, the victory is worth all the pain. I become a hero to myself. God has blessed me, given me a window into His realm. Mihaly, you're right: *Stretch the body and mind to accomplish something difficult and worthwhile.*

BUSINESS

The University of Gold

Am I learning anything new in business? I think not. I've already added new tours to Greece and Scandinavia, a few new dances, a few guitar bookings, a few miscellaneous. Basically, my business is set up. I can't see any big changes. I spent years developing it. Now the only real work is publicizing my events. That's the kind of work I hate. So I will only do the absolute minimum. I've always considered publicity and marketing to be the biggest pain in the ass and, since I don't like a pain in the ass, I hardly do it at all. This is my biggest weakness, but a weakness I accept. The best I can do is hire others to do it. That hasn't worked well, either. I've incurred new expenses by hiring them. Now, instead of hiring them, I exchange services with them. Costs are down, and it works out better. But for now, I can't see any new movement in my business. I'll just keep bouncing it along and concentrate on taking courses at the University of Gold.

Should I add business courses at the university? That would indeed destroy the division between business and study, the artificial distinction between learning and life. It might make business more interesting for me, too. The truth is, I don't mind marketing it if I'm enthusiastic about it. I just have to market it in my own personal way, and my way is a rather unique, mystical way. Basically, I just stand in the corner or center of the room and shine. That is my marketing method: shining. I refuse to do anything else. If any other ideas come along, they come as a by-product, an offspring of that.

Does shining work? How should I know? I'm never really sure why other people do things anyway. They may join my activities *because* I am shining, and they may join them because *they* are shining. Or both. Or for some other reason. But I can't waste my time worrying why other people do things, since I'll never figure it out anyway. I can only figure out why I do—and even that's pretty difficult. My life consists of classes at the University of Gold. It's all inclusive.

Sales and the Triple-F Threat

I wish I could love sales the way Susan Rosenthal does. Mention them, and her face lights up, her eyes dance with joy, and she's heading out the door for the kill. She loves them with a passion. If only I did, too.

Perhaps I don't see it. My envy means part of me wants to sell, even admires sales. Maybe I love sales but hate the word "sales." Sales relate to the two F's: Fear and Force. There's not one word about the third F: Fucking. How would fear, force, and fucking be? The triple-F threat. But fucking is nowhere to be found. Fear and force have pushed fucking out the back door. They freeze and immobilize *me*. Yet people tell me I'm a good salesman. It's true. I couldn't have survived this long in my own business if I weren't. They say I have an honest face and win people's confidence.

Leadership

I am a good tour leader. Why? My mistakes give people confidence. They think, If *he* makes so many mistakes, why can't *I* be a leader, too?

My mistakes give people the freedom to make their own mistakes and survive. Through my example, a life of trial and error, a rocky path strewn with both victories and false starts, I give others confidence to follow their own path.

The Contradictory Joy of a Sore Throat

Is it a sore throat or a cold? Deep down I know it is neither. I got sick to mourn the passing of my tour. I hate mourning. Better to develop a known disease than face the sadness and abandonment of tour loss. Instead of crying through my eyes, I cry through my throat. I want to get down on my knees, cry, sing, laugh, weep, bellow, howl, scream, and run around the room shouting, with tears streaming down my face. Screams will change my life. I need a memorial to this tour.

What's the best one? Renewed commitment.

INVENTIONS

The Nonsense Path

Where does the Nonsense Road lead? No one knows. This unknown path calls me. Doors can open through the unexpurgated writing of nonsense. But walking the irrational Nonsense Path cannot be a goal. Goals destroy the path by making sense. Nonsense travels concealed in darkness; it is often the way of disaster, dynamite, and the devil.

But the road leads to Luminescent Land, where nonsense brightens the day! A walk on the Nonsense Path cannot be plan-ned. Best is to unleash the mind. Let it wander through crisscross fields, dig in hidden hills, unearth secret turnips, ostrich eggs, phosphorescent worms, and rocks pitted with gold.

The Nonsense Path often reveals hidden plans behind the world's apparition.

Marmalade

Today's not a good one. I can feel it. Those leaden weights fastened to my bones dragging me down, pulling me into syrupy seas of fading phosphorous where lily pads eat whale meat and Sarah Fosdick sits on an underwater turnip, chewing tomorrow's cud. How can cows live like that? Is it right? Shouldn't they strive for more dignity? Or is that the nature of a twentieth-century cow? I'm sure Heidegger never had this problem. Did Thomas Wentworth Higgleson? He founded the Sideways Printing Press. Until his invention in 1742, printing was done in circles. Higgleson was also responsible for the sidewards wife. Until 1742, all wives went in circles, following the printing press of their choice. But Higgleson's new invention caused a sensation from Brazil to Bretagne as wives of all sizes, colors, and shapes started going, not only sidewards, but forwards and back as well. It wasn't until the learned King John of Backswitch decided to sail to the West Indies on a stitch that cultural habits changed for the better.

"Isn't is a sin that poppycocks roll backwards?" he asked. "Can anything be done about it?"

The wayward empires of John the Fruit and Lawrence the Mellon, two leading 19th-century romantic grocers, introduced fresh partridge and melon of water into the stirrups of all westward-bound horsemen. After that, America was truly discovered, and bounteousness spread beyond bounds.

Can deviants create history as well as write it? "How can bricks lay hens?" asked John Gathworthy, well-known mental institutionalist, as he fawned on a rope. "And what about parsnips?" If Larry Dunce swims up the Nile, will he reach the Elephantine slopes, or must he sail on to Byzantium? Can the puppet John of Austria really rule the world or can he only rule in the service of a larger puppet?

Big questions, especially for a Saturday afternoon. What would God say about this? Or is He too busy writing Himself? What other friends does He have? Me? Larry and Tom Hartwick? Vanilla Jones and Marble Marmalade? Nancy Pews and Jennifer Lemontree? What about Tom and Judy Snyder? Are they friends, too? Could they read

His letters if He wrote them?

Does God worship Himself? Probably not. No one is that ego-tistical except Peabody Slead, the ice cream man who lives in a cone. He would beat his daughter for a blade of grass. Who can tell what he'd do for a tree?

A wild, mean, savage, uncontrollable beast, that man. Only his wife, Jennifer Slaughter, calms him. She lives in a net and fishes for a living. Salamanders and frogs are her specialty, but sometimes she captures an ant or two. She doesn't give a damn about their civil rights. As far as she's concerned, all insects are the same, and so are rodents.

Oh, sure, you can find a rodent or two that speak French, but deep down they're all the same, all related to Morphet Muffin III, king of rodents and hepplewhites in the upper New York State town of Hurtleville. There, when the coffee juices are singing and the air sockets fill with Heptalian moisture, there's no question that a rocket could arrive anytime soon. Therefore, it's best to be pre-pared.

Caterpillar and dragons are on the march again, too. Hundreds ar-rived for their new line of work—metallurgy. These gigantic night worms dredge the banks of leperhood while casting about for the se-cret of time.

Will Leslie's wings be ready to win the acrobatic contest? Will the syrup of Gooey Stracapostosphere finally work? So many trials have already failed. It is no easy task to reach the stars in a basket.

I'll leave now. You can't call a hog a horse unless its wings are clipped.

GOD

Dry Up?

Will my creative powers ever dry up?

God calls out the words, filters them through my mind, hands, and fingertips, and into the computer. What part of me is transcendent? Right side, left side; front, back; eyes, ears, nose, or throat?

Transcendence is unseen and unheard; it exists beyond touch, taste, and smell. . . even beyond thought. When I vanish in a spasm of death, my transcendence will hover over my corpse, laugh, and move on.

Where it will go—on a tour of distant galaxies, a vacation on a beach in another universe, or into another body? But I will always be in touch with it through my writing, as its energy in verbal form travels through my hands. My creativity will never dry up. How can it? It is part of the universe. Even the *thought* of it doing so is part of the universe.

I Need Miracles!

I need miracles! What better "proof" that God exists than a miracle? But my training, my upbringing, tells me that miracles are ridiculous. No such thing. An illusion. Yet when I heard the Beethoven symphony at age thirteen and suddenly, for no reason at all, broke down crying over the majesty and magnificence of it, *that was my first miracle*. And I've been experiencing miracles ever since. I haven't *called* them that, but it's what they are.

Many miracles fill my life, which itself is one. Certainly writing these pages is a miracle. The writing process happens miraculously. How else can you explain it? Training, language, culture, all count for much. But after that, what or who puts it all together so I can sit down at my computer and let the words fly?

Miracles put me in touch with the Great Ineffables like glory, power, transcendence, beauty, and creation. Ultimately, these are all beyond explanation. Attempts to explain such states usually serve only to trivialize them. Scientific explanations rely on causality: Understand the effect by examining the cause. And this is good up to a (small) point. But the beauty of a deed is beyond causality. Do we really know why we did it? We know how, or what, and can even give a few rational, purposeful explanations. But the ultimate Why? The ultimate

How? These cannot be explained merely through cause and effect. There is a higher power, a transcendent force, running the world. Language and science can only infer it, speak of it metaphorically, but can't explain it. That is fine; that is the way it should be. Too much hubris diminishes and, ultimately, destroys us. Man is meant to be a miracle in the making. We'll settle for nothing more. Why trivialize ourselves through constant psychoanalytical, biological, cultural, historical, and other explanations? Why take away our spiritual strength by diminishing our vision? Our subjectivity gives us strength; we know ourselves like no one else. Self-confidence in our little quirks makes us strong.

Man Is Not Alone, by Abraham Heschel, is a religious, literary, poetic, and theological masterpiece. Some books "are," some books "will be," some books "were," but this book is.

How to react to the God experience? Wonder, awe, and helplessness before the higher Force.

CURRENT EVENTS

Watching TV Diminishes Me

We saw *Schindler's List* last night. Everyone should see it. Words cannot describe such a horror. What a public service Spielberg has performed.

It made me reflect on the power of movies and television. Almost without fail, whenever I go to the movies or watch television, I end up feeling slightly depressed. This has been happening since I was a teenager. Why? Does anyone else feel like me? I've never heard that at all except in a book called *Four Arguments Against Television.* When the movie is over, when the TV is turned off, with very rare exceptions I feel unhealthy. Is it the power of the medium? The images of TV, combined with the hypnotic glare of illusory movements, somehow diminishes me. In the end, I feel weakened and apathetic. It's a vague depression, like a heavy cloud, intangible, difficult to describe. I get no support or confirmation of my feelings when I describe them to others. No one sees it my way. Could I be so far from the mark, so removed from the modern world that, even while everyone watches and seemingly enjoys movies and TV, I actually hate them? I hate the *art form*. It robs my imagination with its impersonal cold power. Maybe it's simply the low caliber of most of the stuff I see on TV and movies; but I think it is *the medium itself*. It mesmerizes and overwhelms me; it moves so fast, I cannot think.

Actors take a risk in live theater; they create right before your eyes. At any moment, they can make an error or create the magic of human enlargement. They're taking chances. TV and movies can always do another take.

I'm still moving around the edges. I can't put my finger on why watching TV and movies diminish me. But they do.

April-June 1994

WRITING

James Joyce

Finnegan's Wake keeps bothering me. I can't even read the damn thing. Why is Joyce so incomprehensible?

Yes, that he could spend years writing page after page of nonsense is a literary tribute to nonsense. Still, if he can do it, why can't I? Even though I can't understand what he's saying, *Finnegan's Wake* had opened a door for me. Perhaps understanding is not as important as example.

Art, Passion, and Writing

Lack of confidence has been a roadblock to my dreams. It has prevented me from admitting how much I love music, writing, and studying. If I do, I'll want to commit myself to them with all my heart and effort and soul.

I have no feel, by contrast, for political oratory. Perhaps deep down I know that most of it has only divided people, and that the arts are the ultimate unifier. People dancing in the folk dance circle don't have time for political arguments. Although I love to listen to political battles from the sidelines, I rarely join in. You never win. Discussing politics is like discussing religion; nobody gets convinced and everybody ends up fighting each other. Politics rarely unites people.

But art does.

In my high school and college years I felt musically and intellectually lacking. What I lacked in skills and abilities I made up for in fervor and enthusiasm. No question, I loved music, my studies, the study process, sitting down at my desk to explore the wonders of the world with book in hand. I circled the universe and traveled through unexplored realms. Ah, a wonder. I loved it, though I only got C's and D's in my tests. What kind of encouragement was that? I never got good marks. I was great at wondering, enthusiasm, and fervor; I just couldn't do well on tests. I lacked confidence, but not love.

How could I stand up or compare to the great artists I worshipped: Heifetz, Casals, Horowitz, Milstein? And of course the thought
of writing music after hearing Beethoven was absolutely out of the
question. I grew up surrounded by clouds, among gods I didn't dare
approach. I felt inferior. But I was constantly aware of the brilliant sun
above me. I had the vision of transcendence, but my vehicles were
thwarted. A music career was unthinkable—my gods had taken care
of that—and intellectual thought and academia were unapproachable
because of my test grades. But since nobody had ever tested or ques-
tioned my enthusiasm and love of learning, they remained intact.

   Writing seemed a perfect compromise. First, I had no prior training in it, no vision good or bad to distract, discourage, or encourage
me. No one in my family had ever been a writer. It was virgin territory.
I liked virgin adventures. In addition, writing combined all my loves:
music through the sound of the words, and intellect through the meaning of words themselves. Writing was a perfect vehicle. I discovered
this new direction during my last year at the University of Chicago.
Upon graduation, I moved to Greenwich Village in New York City,
rented an apartment on St. Marks Place, and spent my time trying to
write a great American novel like my hero, Thomas Wolfe.

   I had sat reading Look Homeward Angel on the subway. Wolfe
had such passion in his writing. I got lost in the swirling flow of his
book, the passion of words I later found out he wrote on top of the
refrigerator, and missed my stop. Nothing got in his way. He wrote on
and on, hour after hour, in a white heat, an unyielding torrential passion like the one I used to feel playing violin concertos in my room.
Nothing could surpass it. I wanted more of it, wanted to devote my
life to feeling and experiencing it. There was a reason to live; it made
a burning life worthwhile. It was my guideline, light, hope, and ever-
present sun, rep-resent ing meaning, purpose and beauty all in one.

   Often the vicissitudes of life hypnotize you. You forget your passion and wonder why you're living it in the first place. I forgot for days,
months, years. During those desert wasteland marches, I longed for
my oasis. I knew something was missing; I had lost my center, identity,
and reason for existence. Yet I was helpless to change course, destined

to cross the desert before my passion burned again.

Am I ready to take it up now? I feel a qualitative change coming. Priorities are falling into place.

Pathways to Radiance

This morning's gray day is penetrating my den—my mind, too. I feel a compulsion to finish an hour of writing, turn out four pages. I push myself to accomplish the task. Otherwise I feel in-complete, as if the day has otherwise been wasted.

This compulsion is genuine. Why? First, I'm afraid I'll dry up, wake up with nothing to say, that my ideas and efforts will have disappeared and I'll become a dull mass of floating protoplasm. This fear demonstrates lack of faith in the creative process and my own powers—ultimately, in the higher powers. Such fumbling with faith pushes me to write. I drive myself into a creative pigpen where I slosh and roll in the mud, bang my head against the wooden walls, and, for an hour, do what feels unnatural but necessary.

Deep down, though, I also know I can reach transcendence through the writing process, attain what James Joyce calls "aesthetic arrest," cast my veil beyond maya and touch the cosmic essence of life, the real purpose and meaning of my existence. Often I rise from writing feeling loftier: I have become worthy again through my actions.

Is that what aesthetic arrest can do? Is it aesthetic arrest when I am not arrested? I am nowhere near resting. Moving, moving, writing, writing, sending my brain rolling down the verbal cataracts. Movement, conflict, the never-ending battle of words clashing, sentences rubbing against each other and producing sparks and ascension. Perhaps when I am finished, arrest will come. God created the world in six days; on the seventh, He rested. Gazing upon His creations, did He experience aesthetic arrest? Not until the seventh day, when He gave us the Sabbath so we too can rest and meditate upon the larger purpose of our existence.

What of maya, the illusion beyond day care?

Is there a higher purpose than art?

There is—the Radiance of Zohar, transcendence, violin playing, a Beethoven symphony.

Art is a bridge to reach the Radiance.

Here is the answer to sinking, bone-deep hopelessness, the dark cloud that appears when I trust my hopes for happiness to the forms of this world. Then I realize they are merely forms, temporal paths to the Radiance. When I confuse the two, I sink deep into the Sea of the Lost. Cataclysmic waves sweep over me, washing away hope, leaving me paralyzed in a darkness beyond death.

Could such darkness be a subtle pathway to Radiance?

I Am the Christopher Columbus of My Mind

I'm afraid to look back, afraid to edit, afraid my words will cease to flow. Is this a common fear? Do other artists suffer from this or is it only me? Am I protecting my creative core when I refuse to look back? Or is it something else?

Maybe my instincts are right; if I review now, I'll kill my creativity and flow. I'm following my instincts. They tell me, not to turn back, but to move relentlessly forward towards this new land I am exploring, a land no one has ever visited before.

I am the Christopher Columbus of my mind. I've set sail, hoping to discover the new world. Will it happen? Is my uncharted approach correct? Will my scattered daily route, rising and falling on meandering waves of stream-of-consciousness journal writing, lead me to the new America?

Deep down I know it will. And deeper down, I know there is no choice. It's the method for this period of my life, a path given me by a superior force, and I must follow where it leads. I must accept no editing or looking back as a weakness, at least for now.

My job is to forge ahead into the darkness—pushing aside the brambles and overgrowth, uprooting trees, wading through swamps while I try to avoid patches of quicksand, staying afloat in a stormy sea—and to keep my ultimate adventure into the unknown alive.

No one can tell me where it leads. I can't read about it or ask others. I can't even ask myself. No doubt something lies out there; some kind of destiny has already been written. What is it? Do I really want to know? Once I do, will I lose interest?

Research and development are based on the hope something useful and saleable will be found. But there are no guarantees. It could all lead to nothing. Journal writing is my personal R and D department. Keep at it!

My Journal Is My Guide

My journal is my guide: I'm posting my schedule on a bulletin board, a list of things to do peppered with philosophies of life to consider.

If my journal is my guide I'll want to read it. It won't represent the dead past but the vibrant future.

A Little Pain

I write better when I am somewhat uncomfortable. You need a little sting of pain, of misery and discomfort, to push the creative effort. The blood has to boil a bit.

Paradox

I have several plans in mind. They are sure to kill any desire to accomplish them.

As soon as I hear a plan, it turns into a must. Then I vanish into won't. Too bad. I wish I were different, but, since I'm a paradox, I'm happy that I'm not.

Barry read my journal in class yesterday. He loved it, and so did everyone else. I was moved. Can I take all these compliments? Will they distract me, inhibit me, prevent me from exploring further? I'm on the verge of new discoveries. I don't want success, which I'm so unaccustomed to—or failure which I'm so used to—to deter me from my goals. Keep my eye on the prize, the swinging ball of transcendence.

It's better to write shit than write nothing at all.

It may fertilize something.

If I write, I don't feel wasted. I've tried, made an effort. Effort wakes me up and relieves me.

The words are flowing faster and easier. It's almost nothing to string out a page or two. My fingers move automatically.

I wanted to improve my writing, develop my skill. This is happening as I write every day, pouring out words, drinking in and spitting out pounds of verbiage. My dream of becoming a writer is being fulfilled.

Notice the words being fulfilled. Notice the word being. It has not been fulfilled, it will not be fulfilled; rather it is being fulfilled. My quest is not over, nor will it be in the future. Rather it is being accomplished in the here and now, in a never-ending process that may be fulfilling but will never reach fulfillment.

Am I a writer? What is a writer? One who writes. Well, I write. Therefore. . . . Scribito, ergo sum. Writing, my active meditation, goes along with running. It's hard for me to sit still. By writing, I run my mouth through my mind. Then its contents dribble out through my fingers onto the page.

I'm reading Paul Brunton again. A wonderful sage. He says, "There are times when writing becomes for me not a profession at all but either a form of religious worship or a form of metaphysical enlightenment. . . . Writing is an act of worship for me." Later, he philosophizes on the meaning of life. "Life remains what it is—deathless and unbound. We shall meet again. Know what you are, and be free. The best counsel today is, keep calm, and aware. . . .The last word is patience! The night is darkest before the dawn. But the dawn comes."

Such great material to think about. It started when I wondered when to begin my writing stint. Should it be after running, yoga stretching, or playing guitar? Should I put it off until I am more awake?

Good questions. But beneath them, Will I succeed? That's the killer. Once questions of success and failure enter my process, I became afraid, and a mini-writer's block develops. I want to make this my form of worship, a religious practice and metaphysical exploration:

a means to an end, not an end in itself.

But to move my writing meditations upward, I will have to give up my entanglements with success and failure, step out of the opposites, enter the realm of One. The mind controls the illusion show. Writing can become a higher form, but it takes lots of practice. When I do it well, my fears disappear and my words flow freely across the computer screen. I just love swimming with the verbal currents.

On Conquering Writer's Block

To be easy, writing has to become a habit like eating breakfast, brushing your teeth, taking a run, going to the bathroom, breathing. But no expectations! Give up all plans of future glory, hopes of recognition, crowds cheering, audiences thronging to read your latest work. Do you have such expectations about brushing your teeth? Do you imagine throngs rushing to your bathroom to witness it? Writing should be approached the same way, as daily fare, a conversation with yourself. This approach takes the fear out of it, makes the process softer, easier. Then, it's like discovering the center of the universe in a loaf of bread.

The Two-Hour Writing Experiment

I'm breaking the one-hour writing barrier.

Is this a good idea? Will I pay for it later by not writing tomorrow because I wrote too much today? Will there be such an equal and opposite reaction?

I am afraid of moving into extreme regions. When you push the natural elements, they usually fight back with a vengeance. Break the barrier, and a new barrier will be created—if not immediately, then soon.

Consider this an experiment to see how far I can go. Should I up my quantity to an hour and a half or two hours? Could I stand it? Or, by pushing harder, will I discover new realms?

I doubt my tour to Turkey will go this summer. If it doesn't, I'll have much of July and all of August off. What better time that to start a new writing experiment?

But then, why not start my experiment now? Two hours of straight time in the morning—with breaks, of course, but an uninterrupted straight two hours.

Do I, though, dare commit myself to write two hours a day, dare make writing my top priority and put everything else in second place? I would be committing myself to a "career" that makes no money. I need to come to terms with that: My "sideline" will become my main work, and my "mainline," my money- making, will become my side line. But at least I be focusing on what's important.

Is that a "higher reason" for losing our folk dance room at Cranbury Chapel last night? Ralph said we're out. At first I felt betrayed. But when I realized I had given it my best fight, I resigned myself to my loss. As I drove home that night at eight instead of the usual eleven, I saw the sun set and said, "How pleasant to drive home early."

Suddenly, I had a wild thought: Some day I might thank Ralph for his intransigence. He was freeing me to do something else. I would write instead. What an amazing thought.

Suppose Ralph is an angel in disguise. God sent him, not only to force me out of my job, but to enable me to rethink and reorganize my use of time and energy. This may be the message in my rejection. I couldn't believe how granite-tough he was; he could not be budged. When I finally let go of the room, I started to admire his absolute resolve. I doubt I could have done it. If someone pleaded, begging me for one more reasonable chance, I would have given in. Not Ralph. I have to look in awe upon his absolute refusal, even though his is not my way and he is a complete asshole.

I have decided on two hours of writing a day, a major commitment. It means my tours, weekends, and folk dance classes will come second. Will I be able to live with such insecurity and inner peace?

I'll have to pray money will come from some unseen source, since I won't be pushing to earn it. Maybe I should take a low-paying job in the post office if all else fails. But as long as I keep the dream alive— write, write, write—it won't be too bad. This means admitting I am a writer. Not a hobbyist, dilettante, or amateur piddling around with phrases. A "serious" writer. Serious is defined in terms of commitment. If my main commitment is to writing, then I am a serious writer.

I've always believed writing to be a lofty goal. Perhaps the time has come to give in to my grand passion and begin my grand search and adventure. Look how events are conspiring to point to my new path: I have no registrants for my Turkish tour in August, so I will be free then to experiment with two hours a day. Now I am not as panicked about the possible loss of my Turkish tour. I'll use my time in another way.

My writing is progressing. Smooth, flowing, and fast. I hope it is clear, too. Hours of practice are beginning to pay off. My fingers fly across the computer keyboard; ideas and thoughts flow almost without effort.

The Glory of Writing

I'm at Solway's, sitting on the porch, writing. I've always wanted to do this. I'll have to learn to use a computer outside. I tried it in Santa Fe, but it wasn't so good. Perhaps the idea of using it outside, with the beautiful sunlight shining down on me, the trees, mountains, green lawns, flowers, and fine air caressing me, is the perfect picture of a writer writing in paradise–but the actuality isn't that great. Maybe you need a beautiful inner scene, not an outer one.

I'm still glad to be here. My entire body aches—no doubt a mirror of my mind, which is aching, too, as it does when my concentration is scattered and I have lost direction. But when I'm focused, my mind is perfect, too.

I might go to Iceland for five days this August. How about adding Norway? A few days in Bergen, a few in Oslo, four or five days in Iceland–a seven-to-ten-day tour alone or with Bernice. I'd like to explore Scandinavia.

What happiness to feel my fingers flying across these keys and feel I'm improving! Could improvement be one of the great unexplored highs?

Paul Brunton says the feeling of disgust with society is an expression of the need for solitude. What a genius he is. I love it. Whenever I feel that way—which is often enough—I'll interpret it as the need for solitude. I can't do anything about changing the world, but I can about getting solitude.

Perhaps I'm short-changing myself with two hours a day of writing. Perhaps I should try three, four, six, or all day. What would it lead to? Madness? Or would I simply run out of gas, fall on the floor, and collapse? Or give up in fatigue and rest?

Maybe I should just write on and on until I drop. That would be an interesting experiment. I'm dropping inhibitions; everything is coming out. If this keeps up, I may not even bother going to Scandinavia. Who has time to plan it? I'll just keep the writing experiment going. This "unleashing" is both within and beyond my control. I fear and I love it. I'm sailing through the stratosphere, over hills, mountains, oceans, valleys, clouds, past winds and moon and sun.

A late afternoon experience. My best times are early mornings and late afternoons. About noon, my mind dies: I need a siesta. I can't do anything after lunch except get depressed, soggy, and miserable because I can't do anything. I can only lie horizontally somewhere. Why fight it? We siesta types ought to stand up for our rights.

God, this is scary. I must be on the right track; otherwise it wouldn't feel so good.

A Crumb of Bread

I am talking about myself.

Is this interesting?

Is this writing?

Is talking about what happened today a good direction to go in? If I merely talk about the mundane, everyday events of my life, will I bore myself and my readers?

Or, in the miserable seeds of every day life, will the kernels of eternity be found?

That's what the Chasids say. Maybe by touching the mundane, particular crumbs of bread on my table, I will indirectly reach the transcendental moments and find union with what Paul Brunton calls the Overself. We'll see. Meanwhile I must move on to bar mitzvah land. I'll take my notebook computer with me, hide it in the car, and try to sneak out whenever I can to write. God bless my notebook!

Writing Miracles

The writing process only offers miracles when I ask nothing from it. When I write with no expectations mental clearing comes as a gift.

A Cup of Espresso and Immortality

Writing words like "resurrection," "messianic age," "messiah," and "immortality" elevate me.

Raised by this supreme kabbalistic view, I travel forward and sideward simultaneously, mingling with stars, comets, touching the dust of angels, inhaling their fragrance and transmitting it. That's the wonder of reading Immortality, Resurrection, and the Age of the Universe, by Aryeh Kaplan.

A cup of espresso coffee make the book fly even further.

My True Home

A dark cloud descended from the sky covered the earth with a fog of hopelessness.

I searched for the god of writing. I hoped to find salvation in the valley of words. I wanted release from the river of despair.

I wanted to climb the luminous mountain. The god of writing smiled and placed his hand on my shoulder. "You are worthy," he said. I felt soothed.

But next day old fears returned: the emptiness, loneliness, abandonment, and hopelessness.

This happened daily for years.

One day the sun smiled down on me. "One day you shall be ready to receive me," it said. "But not yet, not yet.

"One day in the future cycles of millenniums, I shall set my loving foot upon the deserts and treeless pastures of your valley home. On that day you shall be free and rise to me.

"But until that day you must walk in the valley, glancing up-wards, ever yearning for our fruitful and final meeting. Then all pain will run into the valley, float down the dark river of despair to merge and mix in the underworld far beneath my abode.

"You will not understand the nature of your sorrow. Such is my gift to you. It is the freedom to feel despair and hopelessness as you search for salvation and new ways of expansion.

"Only in perfecting yourself will you rise towards me. "I am your true home.

"But you do not yet know me."

The Higher-Calling Job

Is it a writer's job to take dictation from a higher source? Yes. But how often does the source give you a job?

Sometimes you wait in the Higher Calling Line for weeks and months. Unemployment is a constant problem. And the further up the ladder you go, the fewer the calls.

But when the calling comes. . . . Ah!

Meeting Mr. Guilt

I have made the writing process such a habit that, even though I am nervous, I can still write. I can turn out the words no matter how trivial and unimportant they are. My purpose is to turn out page of writing quantity. My personal mandate never said I have to create quality. Thus, simply by moving my fingers across the keys, I am fulfilling my edict.

But I need some guilt to push me. It is my not-so-secret writing weapon. Thank you, Mr. Guilt—I love and hate you.

You want me to reach a higher level. You are unsatisfied with mediocrity. You say, if it is a worthy cause, go for it, give all you've got and then some. You throw away my excuses for poor performance, giving up, and not trying. You push me up Jacob's Ladder straight into heaven.

What's so bad about that? Nothing I can think of.

LANGUAGES

Releasing a Swarm of Mad Bees

Linguistic barriers are falling.

I hear, reverberating in the darkened halls of my mind, a conglomeration of Gallic, Hungarian, Arabic, Czech, Hebrew, Russian, Bulgarian, Turkish, Spanish, French, Italian, German, and English. Add music, art, and ancient languages, birds singing, trees whispering, crocodiles laughing, pea pods stretching, platypuses playing, dinosaur bones rolling, mountains sighing, metamorphic rocks groaning, earth bones cracking, suns rising and creaking upwards on a foggy morning, and more.

Writing this morning is a mysterious sound bath leading everywhere and nowhere at once. I am simply letting the door swing open, pushing down a wall or two. Sounds, trapped for years inside my aural Pandora's box, escape into the atmosphere. I use my finger-and-mind combo in their unending service. I am thankful for becoming a more perfect instrument. It's nice to know I perform a useful function by releasing such a swarm of mad bees on the public.

Goodness Is a Symphony

Goodness is a symphony that makes you cry with the pain of its beauty.

Music cures. I know this.

I write music but use words in place of notes.

Look at my early heros. Beethoven the king, along with Mozart, Mendelssohn, and Pagannini. Others followed. The highest form of creation was to write music. But only gods wrote music. I had to "settle" for so-called lesser forms, that is, playing their music. I could never create it. That would be too high. And too much trouble. Writing down each note, thinking about bars, measures, timings, and instrumentation, restricted me. Basketball had a physical freedom I couldn't find in music. The incredible violin technique you needed before you could "forget yourself" was too great.

Then I went to college and discovered books and, with them, philosophy, physics, history, songs, stories, and a whole new world of transportation through language. This deepened when I spent my junior year abroad in Aix-en-Provence, where I lived, studied, and dreamed in French. The French language became my music, a sonata I could play whenever and wherever I was awake.

Two years later, at the University of Chicago, I was sitting in my room facing 55th Street when I realized that writing combined all I needed: music, intellect, philosophy, language, and poetry. But most of all, writing offered me freedom. I could easily move from one sphere to another. Music and basketball had trained me, but writing was my best personal means of self-expression.

Since college I have known how good writing is for me. But then my Warden of Shit emerged, asking questions: How dare I write, me, a mere beginner, a normal person with minimal if any talent, just a Bronx boy who got C's and D's and an occasional B in class, who played an average violin and average basketball. Average, average. How could I dare put myself in the same constellation as the artistic and intellectual stars I worshiped? Wouldn't it be better to stay on earth with the peasants?

With this attitude, it is amazing I did anything at all. But somehow my low self-image was countered by an unknown force, a voice speaking from a higher plane. "Push on," it said. "Don't take no for an answer."

Luckily I listened.

Did I really have a choice?

As a writer, music is my center—I am composing, not a novel, journal, poem, or story, but a symphony. I cannot think of plot or make long-term writing plans. I grab the moment of music and sing in the here-and-now.

On the Misery of Verbs

Adjectives and nouns are easy to understand, concrete, visible substances. I see, hear, touch, taste, and smell them.

I also understand pronouns.

But I cannot understand a verb. What is it? Where is it? I cannot seize it. Adverbs, too. They are not concrete and visible.

Perhaps it is because verbs and adverbs are floating spirits. I walk slowly is a typical verb and adverb combo. How disgusting it is! I can see the noun walking before me. But I cannot see its verb.

Who are these miserable verbs and adverbs? Why are they so difficult to understand?

Looking Towards Greece and Scandinavia

Whenever I start making elaborate schedules, you can be sure I'm at the end of an energy cycle. It's my way of holding on to the one now fading. But the death of these cycles is inevitable. Better to go with it, follow my inner guides, which are telling me to drop writing for awhile.

Drop writing? Are you crazy? The soul and meaning of my existence? But this clinging is wreaking havoc—writing thrives on freedom, even the freedom to drop it or cut way back.

Meanwhile, my inner guides are leading me to new projects:

Greece and Scandinavia. I must start studying for these tours. Greek, Greek history, mythology, and drama. Scandinavia, too. Do I have the time? Am I taking on too much?

1995 is going to be a very full touristic year. Greece in May, Scandinavia in August, and Santa Fe in late October. I'm skipping Israel for a year, which makes me sad: Am I right? I love Israel. I've put so much time and effort into learning Hebrew. The tour to Israel is my chance to practice. . . .

I've got mucho work to do. The March tours to Budapest and Prague are already set up. Santa Fe, also ready, is an easy tour to run. The real work will go into Greece and Scandinavia. I'll have to learn Greek, then Norwegian, Icelandic, Swedish, even Danish. I'll approach them as one Germanic language.

LIFE

The Rest Is Shit

Since I returned from Budapest I have forgotten almost everything important to me. What happened to beauty, freedom, and my free-flowing, adventurous spirit? I have been crushed by my grasping: for customers, growth, ways of expanding my business.

Why am I bothering with all this? Where did my fresh and innocent vision go? I often rediscover it in the arts and study, my blissful fields. The rest is shit. I should cut back on everything and return to philosophy, metaphysics, poetry, and music. I want to drop my obsession with tour business growth.

Good Deeds as Artistic Creations

When I devote myself to the life of the artist, I am also devoting myself to the performance of good deeds, the moral equivalent of artistic creations.

When I read the beautiful story "The Love of Two Brothers," and the story of Mount Moriah, I cried for its goodness.

I had the same overwhelming feeling of transcendence that I felt when listening to the Beethoven symphony at age thirteen, the same dissolution of ego and melting into the universal that I often feel when experiencing music of great beauty, for beauty is the raison d'etre for life and art.

But now I'm feeling the same response, not to art, but to the performance of a deed of giving. This is the place where beauty and ethics meet, the holy ground of the burning bush. Ethical and artistic beauty come from the same place; they are the same place. Moses was the Beethoven of moral commandments and good deeds, Beethoven the Moses of artistic power.

Aliens Are My Guides

I've been trying to take care of myself all my life with minimal success. When others do, I thrive. I mean the "higher-force" others, unseen aliens from other planets and realms who mysteriously descend to guide me over stormy, windswept seas roaring with dragons. Perhaps these aliens are souls of the dead, or unembodied voices of the living. I don't know who sent them but they guide me through this Stygian misery, along twisted roads, bisecting paths, and major highways.

Telling about My Life

I remember discovering Zen Buddhism in college. What a revelation! Suddenly, I had found a philosophy I liked, one relating to my musical experiences. Feeling oneness in a flash of insight was a common musical experience for me, yet no western philosophers I read had ever commented on it.

Writings on aesthetics, on the other hand, were too intellectual, empty, and off the mark. Somehow the Zen Buddhists just nailed it for me. I was hooked.

I discovered yoga at Chait's Hotel, again by accident. I visited a bookstore in Woodstock and saw a book cover with a man standing on his head. Since I was social director at that time and responsible for programs, I thought yoga might be fun to teach. I didn't know any yoga teachers.

So I decided to become one. I figured I'd read the book, stay a chapter ahead of everyone else, teach the best I could, and see what happened.

I looked at the whole episode an exercise in the art of the absurd, a joke. The idea of a human being standing on his head was ridiculous, my teaching yoga even more so. Perfect! I bought the book and began to study.

Let me digress a moment.

I notice I am telling about my own life. I am an expert on my own life. I know exactly what happened to me. No one can question it or tell me that I'm wrong. No one else has lived it. It's nice to be an expert.

Is this the direction my journal will be going? Will I be drawing experiences from my own life, telling tales of myself? It flows so easily—but it is so revealing. Will it bore a reader?

These questions will be answered in the usual manner. Basically, I'll go in whatever direction I have to go. The Big Voice running my show will point me the right way. When He points, I obey; I have no choice.

The Eubie Diet: Unleashing the Incredible Energy Supply

How long shall I eat myself into oblivion? I should follow the Eubie method: one meal a day. It's more than enough. Sometimes I eat, not because I'm hungry, but to destroy myself. I pile in the food because I can't stand looking at myself—a long-term bad habit.

Can I stop it? Do I dare? If I ate one meal a day, what energy I would have! I am afraid of the energy!

Now I know. I was afraid to find out, but I found out anyway. There is an incredibly powerful untapped energy supply within myself that terrifies me. What would happen if I unleashed it?

Would it destroy or create a new me?
Probably both.

The Irish and the Jews: Qualities of Scholar, Artist, and Fighter

Fighting for myself, inner strength, dignity, standing up, never giving in to what is wrong—I know intellectually that these are great qualities. Most people would be proud to proclaim them.

I, however, am uncomfortable expressing such noble feelings even to myself.

It's time to change my self-image. Evidently, I have always had these fighting qualities—the fighting Jewish-Irish. In my neighborhood, the Irish were the fighters, the Jews, scholars. Jews rarely fought; it was a shande. Only the Irish fought. My mother called them uneducated boors. Later in life, after I ran my first tour to Ireland, I discovered part of me had always loved the Irish—especially that fighting quality. I have both traditions in me. Later, I also discovered that Jews had a long history of fighting tradition going back to the original conquest of Canaan, up through the Maccabean rebellion against Rome, and, of course, in modern times, the founding of Israel.

The Irish, on the other hand, have had a long scholarly tradition dating back to the pagan Druid priests of the early Celtic tribes. The Christian monasteries of the fifth and sixth centuries had their crowning achievement in the magnificent Book of Kells. No one uses the English language like the Irish, who possess an incredible modern literary tradition with beautiful folk songs and dances as well.

Reaching the Higher Spheres

I was brought up as a musician. I often see myself playing violin in my room. Stars, suns, moons, and other celestial forms passed above me as I played Mozart, Wienawski, Beethoven, Lalo, Bruch, and Bach. I still see myself listening to the radio in our kitchen, eating Cheerios, and mentally melting to the inspirational music of Beethoven and

Tchaikovsky on WQXR. Those were my highest moments. The gate opened then; I was ushered into a world where gods dwelt.

Music has always been my center. On violin, and later on guitar, I played other people's music. I was their instrument—loving, willing, but instrument nonetheless. Being governed by their restrictions was an important step in artistic growth. But it wasn't the final one. In college, I discovered the excitement of language and ideas. I never got good marks. Dry intellect never held me. It was the beauty of ideas, the tasty morsels of words, and the rolling language forming in my mouth, that inspired me.

During my last year in the University of Chicago, as I sat in my second floor apartment on 55th Street, I first thought of becoming a writer. Writing had music and beautiful sounds; it touched my intellect as well as my soul. Most of all, it had freedom. When I wrote, I could finally express myself. Classical music, though beautiful, was filled with restrictions— do's and dont's, and endless possibilities of making mistakes. How could I be free when I constantly worried about committing such a crime, or facing the judgement of an audience?

I thought about art. I took classes in sculpture and pottery. But again these forms felt heavy and earthbound. The only form I might like was painting, and, although I never took a class, I did end up studying calligraphy, combining art with my beloved letters, language, and writing. But again, even painting felt limited to a canvas. I was born with a primary sensitivity to sound. That is my bottom line. Beautiful sounds break down my barriers and transport me to higher realms. When I write, I compose a symphony of sound. When I write, I often get a wonderful feeling of fulfillment. I imagine a grandiose plan of destiny, where I was put in the world to write.

Retreat

Before I start anything, I must first retreat, disappear into my cave, climb my mountain, sit far from the world, far away in the desert, and contemplate my life, my direction, my future, my past, my purpose, all the big questions: a summer of retreat.

Can I survive three months alone doing that, without the usual props of regular folk dance classes, weekends, tours, money worries, stock market worries, and all the other work- related, finance-related activities with which I usually fill my mind? I have an opportunity to experiment, to push writing to the limit, to push music and song to the limit, to push running and its concomitant exercises to the limit.

Feeling Good After a Run

I just returned from a fantastic run! The sky opened up and I saw Uncle Himmler guiding his Zeppelin through Macy's department store with a bread basket on his shoulders. Such visions are not commonplace, especially in Teaneck, home of garden sidewalks and soft rye bread. How can I return to normal after such a good run? It takes hours to come down, sometimes a whole day. I'll just ride the waves, sing with the tides, kick my heels in the sun while blue skies sing a Whiffenpoof serenade.

Who would have expected such a run? I started out so leaden, slow, and dead. My legs could hardly move, concrete under my thighs, every inch of pavement a battleground. This sluggish, pusillanimous running went for forty minutes. Then, just at the end, a mere two blocks from my house, a whiff of inspiration descended. Why not add a few blocks? I thought. I ended up adding half an hour, running hills, breathing cool, beautiful air on a most delicious day under a beneficent sun with light falling all around me. Ah! I returned home, took a cold shower, did push-ups, sit-ups, hamstring stretches, shoulder stand, head stand, and some chi kong squats. I didn't realize how glorious I was feeling until an hour later. I sat on the sofa reading about Chinese yoga and how to take a gentle breath, hold it as long as possible, then gently breathe out in order to increase my abstract concentration. The first breath relaxed me; the second brought a delicious sleep.

I awoke after five minutes feeling absolutely great.

Group Meeting

Last night's group meeting was superb. I spoke "like my journal": uncensored. Our group members looked at me in astonishment; I looked at myself in astonishment. I had such a damn good time! So loose, free, saying whatever I thought. I helped Carol and Mark by telling them how much security and fun you could still have in a miserable marriage. I laughed a lot, made jokes, approached the evening with a verbal fuck-it-all attitude. I was proud of myself.

The evening started off with a discussion about nursing homes and retirement residences. How boring can you get! George told of his plans to enter one; Ilsa, his wife, to her credit, didn't want to go. Thank God someone is still alive in that family. Then Carol talked about her mother's nursing home. This went on for an hour. I sank further into my chair, secretly vowing never to attend a meeting again.

Suddenly, the conversation moved to death in general.

This, believe it or not, was a step up.

Soon we were discussing all the ways we could die, or lose all our money before we died. The most pleasant method of extermination was suicide which, as the meeting progressed, I was contemplating more and more.

Bernice went into her routine on retirement—how we have no money, and we'll soon both be old and have no one to take care of us. Against this background, the only purpose I could find to keep on living was to get out of this meeting as fast as I could. Luckily, Bernice forgot to bring Carol's bike. I volunteered to get it—and left.

Confidence

I'm thinking about my newfound strength and confidence.

It scares me. It is so different from my accustomed me. How did it start? With an unshakable confidence. I have moved to a new level in spiritual development. This belief in myself has a lasting quality. It gives me inner peace. . . but it also scares me.

Am I deluding myself? Is it just another form of hubris? I doubt it. I've been preparing for years. I'm ready. I've paid my dues.

It began in January when I decided to apply tough love to myself. I forced myself to do the things that bring me transcendent satisfaction and the feeling I've been put on the earth for this purpose. I've listened to my inner voice, risen to meet my higher self.

My first commitment was to writing. I forced myself to write every day for an hour, or four pages, or both. This was my first discipline. I pushed everything else, including money making, to second place.

From this came other wonderful insights. First, the stock market went down three hundred points, and I lost lots of money. I had been in the stock market for eighteen years. After all those years I'd had some gains, more losses, but overall I still hadn't made any money. Had I simply left my money in the bank, I would have been way ahead. But I love the market, the excitement of gambling, the hope that someday I'll succeed even though the task is close to impossible. But there was a qualitative difference about this market descent: it made me think differently about fate, karma, and destiny.

I concluded I will never get rich. It is my destiny not to make lots of money, so I might as well give up trying. However, it is also my destiny to somehow always get along; even without large sums of money, I'll make it. I'll do the things I want and have to. At this juncture, my fascination with the market descent diminished, but, more important, my self- confidence jumped sky high! After all, if I believe I'll somehow make it through life's travails and misfortunes, that's a golden gift no amount of money can buy. In fact, it's why I wanted lots of money in the first place, as an insurance policy to buy self-confidence, to insure that I'll make it in society through the accidents, sickness, falls, disabilities, and possible financial ruin. But now I owned the insurance policy! The only cost was years of suffering and worry about money. Imagine, I would have made the same amount if I hadn't worried and just done my job!

Could I have found this self-confidence because writing has put me in touch with a higher power? My tough love approach has forced me to sit in its presence every day for one meditative hour. When I write I feel like I am taking dictation. Someone, something, is pushing the words through my fingers and across the keys. I am the instrument. Strange verbs, nouns, ideas, and languages flow through me. It is not so much what I say but the experience of saying it that puts me in touch with this higher power in a kind of mystical illumination I've felt all my life but have never been able to explain.

The decision to write was the decision to accept this higher power into my life on a daily basis. Perhaps it's the source of my confidence.

Ghosts

My fears are blinders put on to hide my energy, to keep me away from my strength, to push me back into the old world of hell, melancholy, and whining, and longing for Mama's big gorgeous breasts, for the patrician hold of money feeding where I can suckle at the tit of security. Away with these miserable fears! I must move forward, onwards, backwards, sidewards, upwards, downwards, beyond the paralysis of the stone-cold fear habit.

The Benefits of a Schedule Crutch

Writing is linguistic music mixed with charcoal and water color images. I paint pictures with musical notes, using letters and syllables for my brush. Plots form as the horizon dims—a dawn beyond dawns, life beyond lives.

In order to write every day, I have created a schedule crutch. Without such a device to give me support, I might simply degenerate and do nothing at all—just eat, sleep, and watch TV.

Am I really so bad? Probably. Never predict how low one can sink. Without structure, there's no telling.

I don't trust myself, and I don't find any reason why I should. The snake of self-gratification lies waiting, ever ready to pull me into the pit where I'll wallow with the other snakes, slithering among the dregs of my inner population of weasels, ants, mice, and other rodents of the garbage family. I could easily fall prey to slithering. My system helps me fight against my miserable self, to fight the piss balls, lumberers, and cesspool men who would drag me down into the quagmire of satisfying every sniveling desire.I have other crutches of even loftier magnitude. How about the impossible-dream crutch? That's a beautiful one designed to raise my sights and push me beyond the possible.

Some people might call crutches 'goals'; others might call goals 'crutches'. Whatever, they are a necessary ingredient in the endless struggle against sloth and decay, as well as the endless search to reach the stars.

Pushing

I've just dumped my psychological guts on the page. I don't feel any better. Dumping may not be enough. Better to push beyond psychological guts.

Pushing is difficult. By striving to transcend the typical barriers of everyday life, I can destroy the dead forms of yesterday, break through, and reach a new level of freshness, elevation, and energy. I can step over the lifeless body of the status quo.

When I push myself in running, I reach new heights; when I push myself in writing, I remove my July 4th Weekend worry and anger; when I push my guitar playing, I end up exhilarated. By pushing my business, I'll end up with customers.

Pushing is the way to go. Breaking barriers, smashing yesterday's forms, moving into the here-and-now of today. Striving and struggle bring the temporary happiness I crave. It's hard work. I hate and love it.

But I have no choice. If I don't push, I get depressed. If I get depressed, I'm forced to do something about it, namely, push. So I might as well start pushing before depression starts.

It's a foggy, dreary day with humidity in the high hundreds. It feels like the day when God created the world. No wonder He created man.

Who would want to live alone in this humidity?

My mental drainage system is working this morning, cleaning out every idea in my brain. I'm sick of everything I've been doing. I need a break.

So I'll take one.

I'll put my books on the shelf and return to my old primordial self, the one I once got such a kick out of. But I can't return to the past even though, at the Music and Art High School reunion, I gave it a good try. My former classmates don't fool me. Here are the stars of today—famous actors, musicians, composers, and ordinary people, too.

My high school classmates have had lives of accomplishment and misery. Yet even though they have done so much they are all still only seventeen years old! They must be wearing masks for the occasion.

Forget the past. The past is the future wearing a disguise.

Improvement as Good-in-Itself

The beautiful smell of improvement haunts the room. It is my wake up call. Improvement elevates me, calls up my energy, wakens the sleeping kundalini serpent coiled at the base of my spine, sends it hurtling through the doors, windows, and exits of my spinal column, upwards into my brain and outwards through my fingers into the guitar, or over the computer keyboard and across the writing page. I need improvement as a goal.

But I fear the word 'improvement.' The mention of it makes me feel inferior. After all, if I have to improve, that means I wasn't that good in the first place. I have to move from lower to higher in order to justify my existence and be recognized by the important others in my personal constellation.

I would rather see improvement as a goal-in-itself, a Kantian Good-in-itself, ultimately unattainable yet an ever present Janus-faced driving force.

Circadian Rhythms

I look at the mornings. I'm doing fine. Then comes the after-lunch dip. It lasts from noon to about three-thirty. By four I'm ready to go.

Sometimes I can push it to three-thirty.

But why push? Why not accept my circadian rhythms? Instead of fighting them, work with them. We know five a.m. wake up is the best. Sometimes I can push it back to four-thirty; sometimes I oversleep to six. Morning reading, followed by writing or guitar playing, then running followed by yoga, a light breakfast followed by a short rest, and a return to either the guitar or writing. This is an okay morning.

Then comes noon. . . and my period of assimilation.

What should I do with it? I don't like giving in to my circadian rhythms. Should I do so or push myself?

Questions

Have I been here before?

Is this a continuation of another life? Did I know Bernice long ago? Were we married once before? Has she always been my wife but in other bodies? How about my family? Have we all been here before?

Was I playing guitar or a similar instrument long ago? Why do I have an affinity for stringed instruments and not winds? Did I always have children? What about my grandchildren? Who are they? Have they always been related to me? Did I know them once before in Egypt, the land of Canaan, or in 16th-century Westphalia?

Did I have these questions centuries ago? Are they long-term concerns or ones I am simply working out in this life?

Passion and isolation.

My passion sometimes frightens me. I can accepts parts, little pieces, big pieces, short times, long times, but to give in to it completely, to follow it to the limit, that is something I am afraid of. How far can I go?

If I follow my passion, will I lose my friends? I could also lose my family. I'll lose everything and everyone who is important to me.

On the surface that seems like a good reason to avoid giving in to my passions. But, truth is, if I restrain myself, I wind up leading a half life. Worse, when I face my Maker and He asks, "What have you done with your existence?" I'll have to admit that I didn't work at my most worthy task—the fulfillment of my talents. How can I face death saying I didn't give life my very best shot? Better to have lost all friends and family if that's the price I must pay to follow my passion. What kinds of friends are they anyway if they would leave because I followed my calling and gave my talents my best shot? I'd be better off alone. I don't mind the isolation.

Island Life

My masters are collapsing.

I want to kneel at their feet, to yield to their hands, and bask in their love. But, alas, what do they know about me? What can they know? For although they are masters, they are still not me. Only I can know me.

I am my own master. I live alone on a separate island, sending out throaty calls, waving to other islands around me, and, on occasion, even visiting them. But I always return.

The masters, too, live on islands. They may have better boats, better planes, more throaty calls—but these are merely technical improvements. They can never know life on my island, since only I live there.

Sadly I must give up my hope for masters. None can save me. I am a university of one, studying and graduating on my island home. My diploma may bring me a new and better boat and even sunglasses if I am lucky. But no matter how many degrees I receive, I will always be a prisoner on my island, with only the possibility of temporary work release.

There are positives. First, I can't take criticism by others very seriously. After all, they only see things from the perspective of their islands. How useful or true, really, is their criticism? I may agree with them, disagree, or remain indifferent. The only power in their criticism is the attention I pay to it. Islands can never fully communicate to each other anyway. But they can send messages and wave a lot. As the 17th-century poet John Donne said, "No man is an island." But at least he can do his own gardening.

Withdrawal

I am withdrawing. Whether this lasts all summer, all year, or for the rest of my life, I do not know. I do not want to be bothered by anybody or anything. I only want to write, play guitar, run, and study—in that order.

I takes courage to withdraw, especially when the withdrawal is confirmed with no bookings, registrations, checks in the mail, or phone calls. Business is dead. It is what I want for a summer of withdrawal but worrisome. Is my business withdrawing, too? Without money from it, I will not be able to withdraw too much longer.

It's an old story. Only courage and faith in a higher power will keep me from worrying. Hopefully, I'll return from withdrawal as a wiser person. That, after all, is the purpose of retreat.

MONEY AND ITS BRETHREN

The Courage to Grab It

Why am I wasting my time trying to make a living? "Working" is a hideous thing, something I should avoid at all costs. Why struggle against my instincts and beliefs?

Why do I feel so sick and lost?

Truth is right in front of me: I only need the courage to grab it.

I should follow my vision, give up hopes and the scramble to make lots of money. I don't believe in money, only in the security it can bring. The desire for it only begets desire for more. It does not loosen my mental shackles, does not lead to focus, peace of mind, and the challenge of purpose I need to be an artist.

Of Means and End

Am I smart! I always knew, if I ever removed my fears of financial ruin, I would find hundreds of other fears. Pandora's box would open, and out would pop a stream of cloudy dragons and faceless demons. Financial fear was merely the lid. My narrow focus on money freed me from dealing with them.

Yet I've always made it, even though finances are and have been precarious. Why not believe in myself? Wouldn't it be better to focus on the higher forces that keep me in place? Why continue this never-ending worry about money?

Well, I've come to the end of my agony. The fear of financial ruin is easing back.

And sure enough, new black doors are opening.

I woke up this morning almost paralyzed with nameless fears. Slowly concerns coalesced: I'll be unable to teach folk dancing or play the guitar. I could get an incurable disease at any moment or be over-whelmed by my unfulfilled talents, the creations I should have made, must somehow make, but don't have the time to. So physical and psychosomatic fears have replaced financial ones.

Do they all boil down to lack of confidence?

This journal is turning into a personal psychoanalysis. Oh, no, not again! I'm sick of psychoanalysis; I can't stand looking at myself any-more. Is there no end to this self- absorption? But what can I do? I must write what I must write. Today it is this.

But good things are coming out, too.

I started reading The Agony and the Ecstasy, by Irving Stone. What a pleasure to read about the life of Michelangelo! I haven't read a novel for years. Why? They're so involving, I lose myself in them and forget my work, my financial cares; forget to write, play guitar, call for bookings, think about tours, weekends, folk dancing, and getting more customers; forget about business, survival goals, and purposes. I lose myself in a beautiful story, merge with a great idea.

Reading a novel is a wonderful experience I have denied myself so I could be free to concentrate on ancestral fears of financial ruin. The same is true of symphonic music.

It's the price I have paid for freedom, entrepreneurship, and self-sufficiency.

Not a bad price—I won't complain about it—but the price structure is changing; I'm moving into a new market of artists, novels, music, and transcendental spheres, taking another step towards knowing what I want and who I am.

Doing what I want is possible when I'm ready to do it.

Back to origins!

What was the original purpose of my tours? To experience first-hand how folk dancers in other countries danced. I wanted to know the creative limits of my own choreography. How much could I improvise? How far I could go? How creative could I be and still stay within folk traditions? What were folk traditions, anyway? After years of running tours to Hungary, Czechoslovakia, Israel, Bulgaria, Greece, Ireland, Egypt, and Turkey, I found out. In the process, I became a stronger teacher, learned to lead tour groups, and improved my business skills.

Then a quantitative goal formed: I wanted to run tours to thirteen European and Middle Eastern countries, develop a multimillion-dollar business, and sit at home collecting oodles of dollars while other people ran my tours, doing most of the work. How did I arrive at such a vision? Means turned into an end. My original goal had been to develop as folk dancer and teacher. Slowly, this degenerated into one of bloated economic security flavored by greed. Pursuing my artistic and intellectual interests wasn't enough. I wanted more, more, more! I pigged out. I wanted money for its own sake.

And, almost as if to teach me through divine punishment, as my desire for wealth expanded, my expenses grew and my income diminished. Soon I was in big debt.

Worrying about money was killing my art. I hoped the stock market would help me achieve economic security.

Then I could lead my life as an artist in financial peace.

Soon, however, making money in the market became a goal in itself. The means had metamorphosed into the end. I was sure I could beat the system.

But after years of small wins and losses, I ended up about even. In reality, I lost.

Had I simply put money into low-interest-bearing accounts, I would have had more than I'd started out with. Now I must admit my seventeen-year stock market adventure is a failure—fun, fascinating, dynamic, but financially a failure. It's no fun if you don't win. You feel like a fool who has lost money, time, and expended mucho mental effort for basically nothing.

This is the downward path when means metamorphose into ends.

Road and Goal Are One

Road and goal are one. As soon as I start out, I am there.

It's taken eighteen years of losses to figure it out: the stock market is for fools. I'm a graduate of the University of Financial Loss. I've paid for my education dearly. I can't remember how many thousands of dollars I have lost in the vain hope that someday, through financial success, I'll be saved from the insecurity and vicissitudes of life. I'm disgusted—but I'll vomit in the sewer and go on.

PERFORMANCE

Duty and Guitar Performance

Is it my duty to perform my guitar shows? I wish it were. Perhaps some day my wishes will come true. What a shame I no longer want or need to "share my talents" with an audience. I hate/love to perform and have given it up. I don't even believe it's a shame. It's a relief.

I used to try to figure out what the audience wanted. I gave up the reins and handed over the horse. "What do they want?" thinking became a habit that sapped my power; it made performing a torture from which I have yet to recover. I still play guitar. But now it's alone in my room. I love it—so peaceful, elevating, fulfilling, and relaxing. I don't want to lose my love, throw it away playing for audiences and giving in to my old habits.

What a shame I can't hold on to my love and play before an audience. But then I will have to take the chance the audience will walk out on me.

That is my fear: They will leave. That will "prove" that I am no good. I don't believe this anymore, but these were my old thoughts. Could I develop new ones, get in front of an audience again and, instead of "performing," delve deep into my love of music, tone, sound, elevation, beauty? What a conquest that would be.

I would have to think differently when I play guitar.

Nothing fails like success; nothing succeeds like failure. I aim for success, yet when I achieve it, I get depressed.

Witness what happened in writing class.

Barry read my journal. He loved it.

So did the class.

So did I. At last I was a "serious" writer, admired and respected. What could be better?

I went home elated. But next day my motivation and energy drained away. I sank into a post-success low.

All this is nothing new. It happens over and over again. Some day I hope I can give up this failure/success syndrome. Concentration on success and failure sap my primary motivational force, my love of beauty. What can I do? I'm sadly human.

Returning to Destiny and Performance

This morning I practiced guitar in the Solway living room. A wave of peace swept over me. I listened to the beautiful tones wafting out of my guitar during one moment of solitude. I thought again about renouncing the world, becoming a hermit, and dwelling in some mountain cave away from all the worries and cares of this world.

Suddenly, an old vision of an audience invaded my mind. I put myself in performing mode. Tension. Worry. My mind leaped from inner peace to performing turmoil. Then I realized I cannot escape my audience! They will always be with me, in reality or imagination; they are my destiny, responsibility, and burden. Moses on Mount Sinai fell on his knees, pleading, "Lord, Lord, don't choose me. I can't lead my people. I am too weak for this. Besides, I have a stutter. Please let me go home to lead a simple life and learn Chinese cooking."

But Moses knew his destiny had been written, his mission decided, even before he was born.

Could my mission have been decided before I was born? Has my destiny been written? Is it only a question of opening my eyes to discover it?

I have avoided performing for years. But no matter how I tried, I could never get the audience out of my mind. They pursued me in private practice, and especially whenever I picked up the guitar. I could not elude them.

Maybe I can change my attitude. Instead of denying my audi-ence, I'll include them in my practice.

Last night when I returned from folk dancing I switched on WQXR-FM and heard a live performance by the New York Philharmonic of Beethoven's "Fifth Symphony." The Fifth is better than Barry Gray, Rush Limbaugh, Curtis Sliwa, or any other talk show.

Then I thought about translating its overpowering images into my guitar playing as I played this morning.

Every time I play a piece, I have to do it differently, improvise around the given notes, interpret them, change the nuances, play them faster or slower. I must create while playing. What I am communicating to the audience is on-the-spot creation Hungarian style.

It's hard to verbalize the guitar and performing things that are happening. Words seem awkward, pale. Imagine, returning to performing. I can't believe it.

As I sang "J'ai Rendez-Vous Avec Vous," then "Drill, Ye Tarriers, Drill," I couldn't believe how well I was doing it. I even threw in blue notes, quarter notes, and a mellow bass tone.

Bob Waite called. We'll have lunch together tomorrow. I haven't seen him for a year. In fact, I've hardly seen any friends for a year. I've been hibernating, retreating, involved in my work, cherishing whatever free time I have. Friends, unfortunately, come last.

It's ten o'clock, and Dennis Prager is on WABC. He has raised the level of that station one thousand percent. I've rearranged my schedule around his one-hour program. I wish they would take him off the air so I would be free from ten to eleven.

As I sat on the toilet eating stew, I opened the Stone Ridge Cultural Co-op Newspaper to the Gemini advice in the astrology section. "You are one of the Zodiac's prime communicators. . . . Be aware that you must focus on one particular area and not try to do it all. Keep up with your exercises and dietary regimens; they will help you remain on target."

What does this astrological advice mean? Why did I read it in the first place?

Today was a good beginning. I started out at 6:00 a.m. with coffee and twenty minutes of Hebrew, then practiced the guitar beautifully for an hour; I followed this with a half hour of songs. What exquisite physical pleasure in producing good singing tone. As I pictured myself performing such luxurious throat vibrations, I thought, Is it legal to have so much fun playing guitar in public? Without my usual barriers, won't I simply descend into the public fun pits and enjoy myself to unheard of proportions until I am arrested by the fun police? These questions have never come up before.

So much fun in one morning, merely by playing the guitar and singing. If this what my future holds, what will I do for pain? How will I get in my daily portion of suffering?

Yesterday was a big success. Guitar, songs, writing, running, even lunch with Bob—all a big success.

Except for the dizziness. Why the dizziness?

It came from fear of the higher realms. Yesterday I had briefly entered the higher realm.

Exotic, breathtakingly beautiful, a full panorama of bliss lay before me. I kept holding my breath; the higher realms frightened me. Too much beauty can break the bones; an overabundance of light can shatter the vessel. You must be ready to ascend. Otherwise it can be dangerous. Climb Jacob's Ladder too quickly and you're heading for trouble.

My breakthrough day frightened me. It was too much fun. Could I stand it? Would the fun police take me away?

What a strange paradox. You work all your life to reach the higher realms, and when you get there, it scares you so much you back off.

This morning is my back-off morning. But I ask: What better way to spend my time than the way I spent it yesterday? It may have scared me, but that doesn't negate its truth.

In the process of going after my goals, I get scared. Well, so what? Scared is part of the game. In fact, it may be good. Worries protect me from staying too long in the higher realm. Too long a stay might imbalance, even destroy, me.

My Invisible Audience

Poetry, as Yeats said, is "a high and lonely profession." Yet, deep down, I believe someone is listening to me. But I'm not sure who. I am being read even as I write.

So why publish? My invisible audience may be enough. It may be the only audience I ever get. It may also be my only real audience.

It feels like it is one person, an "entity."

Is that who I am writing and performing for? I believe it is.

Sucking Honey from a Phrase

Sitting on the front lawn of the farm, I played a slow, beautiful, easy "Leyenda" followed by "Prelude Number 4" by Villa-Lobos.

I had given up all notions of speed and technical prowess. Peering into each note, drawing out the essence, sucking honey from each phrase, with never a thought to speed, no shadow of Segovia or Julian

Bream hanging over me, or of a critical audience judging my playing, I discovered another key to my performing future. It was: give up the idea of performing.

But what does that mean?

It means moving a step closer to merging my writing with my guitar playing. My writing experience is spontaneous, not audience bound. No one is looking over my shoulder, criticizing me, and that is because I write without an audience in mind. I do it simply because I love the process. If an audience happens to show up, fine. But pleasing them is not my ultimate purpose is writing.

I'd like to think the same way playing guitar. I'm on the cusp of a new approach.

As I sat on the lawn playing, I imagined the audience in front of me, yet my mind was not on them but rather on creating new meanings and adventures within the notes. "Leyenda," "Prelude No. 4," "Alhambra," Bach, were my raw materials to build and explore new worlds.

I Am the Audience

Where is the audience?

Who is the audience?

I am the audience. The audience I imagined so clearly at the Klezmer Solway Weekend was none other than myself. I had pictured a more substantial one of flesh and blood occupying chairs in front of me, looking me over with jaundiced eyes, critical mien, and a crumb or two of love.

They were outsiders, foreigners sitting passively, waiting for me to please them.

I had been trying to avoid them for years. But I made peace with them on the Weekend. "I'll give in," I said. "I'll accept this damn audience. I'll never get rid of them anyway. I might as well play for them." But this morning I realized I was the audience! Imagine that! I am playing for me. The audience "out there" is my creation. I imagine them into existence.

Transcending Speed

I had another guitar breakthrough this morning. I transcended speed, dropped my bondage to images of Segovia playing "Alhambra" and "Alard" at lighting speed, or Julian Bream whizzing through "Leyenda." God, it was exciting when they played!

I've been trying to play like that for years with no success. Much as I try, I can't. Theirs is not my path. Better to discover my own way.

Isn't it about time? Of course. But art can't be rushed. When my creations are cooked, the bell will ring.

It rang this weekend. Good-bye, Bream, Segovia, Sabicas, Montoya, and Serrano. Good-bye, my ancient heroes who played so beautifully but made my life so miserable by giving me an inferiority complex which has taken years to shake.

Of course, I wanted my inferiority complex. Evidently, I needed to humble and torture myself so I could slowly climb the ladder of writing and, ultimately, return to my guitar playing.

Writing and music blending together in a pas de deux partnership. It's coming.

My first step is transcending speed.

Getting the Notes Right

The audience is always watching. I've got to do what's right. Aha, a moral law! I've found the Torah right in my own back yard!

I interpret "what is right" as playing good honest notes on my guitar. No wonder I'm afraid to perform. One stumble, and I'm on God's shit list. Each wrong note is a moral failure, each missed one a big mistake.

A few of those, a forgotten phrase, and I slide off the road for a quick descent into hell.

Roaring from the Mountain Top

Last night Mal Stein invited me to do a reading along with Bob Waite at the Bergen County Poets group. My first reaction was, "Not me. I don't have the time or interest for it." Then I thought again. Why not me? Perhaps it is time. I had just decided to start sending out my writing. A few hours after I made the decision, Mal called with his offer. Then came the Bobsey twins, excitement and fear. Mostly fear. I imagined myself standing before the audience, reading my work, hoping for approval, fearing negative judgements. I've been so through this countless times before, I'm sick of this reaction.

I know my work is the best I can do. I even know I don't know myself; and if I don't, how can the audience?

Still, my fear of the audience is a personal choice. In the past I have chosen to accept it.

Now I am ready to move forward by trading fear for self-confidence. In order to be unafraid, I have to accept the possibility of ostracism and loneliness. That's not so bad. What's wrong with ostracism? It gives me lots of time to be alone, meditate, and work. As for loneliness, well, it has the same benefits as ostracism.

On the mountaintop of self-confidence, I can roar like a lion even though I may be roaring alone. The denizens in the valley below may not even hear my noise. And there are benefits to performing on a mountain top—the view, and the proximity to the sun's heat.

These are marvelous pluses.

BUSINESS

The Secret Nature of Art

Apollo was the god of music, poetry, and medicine.

Music and poetry are the medicines that cure body and soul.

I often rediscover this truth as I play guitar, write, or dance. Last night I rediscovered it teaching folk dancing.

The evening started out slowly. By seven o'clock only two people had shown up. Another losing night, I thought—no money or people. But soon the regulars came. The music, the small but knowing community of folk dancers, moved together, creating a lovely evening of peace and satisfaction.

Maybe I should keep my dance classes a secret. Give up on advertising. If more people come, great, but if not, that's not so bad either. Perhaps I was not put on the earth to make money but to bring beauty to others by bringing it first to myself. Making money has nothing to do with that. But there is something else going on here that I have sensed for years but never been able to verbalize: The secret nature of art, the transcendent experience which cannot be verbalized, at least by me. When I try, I usually trivialize it. I must sense this killing technique deep down within me, for I have always resisted telling about my events. I cannot advertise myself or what I am doing. I end up joking and fooling around. I never go directly to the point, because, deep down, I'm afraid that, if I try telling about it directly, I'll kill it. The hidden aspect keeps it alive for me.

This holds true, not only for the arts, but for my tours, weekends, and dance classes as well. It probably holds true for just about anything good I do, since the art experience is central to my nature, fundamental to my personality.

I can't talk about sex, music, writing, even history. Talking kills. I doubt I can talk about anything spiritual, bring it down to the verbal, "explainable" level. How can you describe Shining, or its reflection in shining eyes? Only metaphors work. That's probably why I use the indirect approach; a frontal attack can easily be deflected, whereas a back-door approach may help me gain entrance to the castle. Art and business, transcendence and commerce, do not mix. Render unto Caesar what belongs to Caesar, and render unto Me what belongs to Me. I can see no other way.

Have I given up? Yes, I have. The phone has stopped ringing, checks have stopped coming in the mail, all my events and registrations are down. As soon as I am certain about something, the opposite begins to happen. Summits of enthusiasm and hope always lead down the backside of the mountain to bottomless pits of despair, which, in turn, lead to the towering tops of the next mountain. Man is a paradox. I am a leading example. I can hardly believe anything I say, because as soon as I say it, its opposite takes over. Such is the life of a Gemini.

Witness my argument against advertising and business. The "I am an artist" concept, although true, is again running into its opposite, the businessman/entrepreneur's. It's happening because I'm getting angry! Yes, angry, because nobody is calling me, because checks and registrations are not arriving in the mail and my folk dance classes are off. Soon I'll pop, return to business with a vengeance, and fight for my events, classes, and loves. I've been sick and rolling downhill ever since my meeting at Scanam Tours. The downwards blast in the stock market didn't help either.

Perhaps I just needed a rest. Well, I've gotten it.

The Best Sales Technique Is Prayer

Is God knocking at my door?

Yesterday I opened the refrigerator door, and a pot of chicken soup fell out and spilled all over the floor. I screamed, stamped the floor, then smashed the refrigerator with my fist. Bernice said, "I've never seen you get so angry at a person."

I answered, "Damn this refrigerator! No one is registering for my events. Business has been dead for over a month. I've cancelled my Bulgarian tour; the Turkey tour is about to be cancelled, too. The July 4th Weekend and Smorgasbord Weekend have two people registered. My stocks are down. I'm almost broke. I'm mad as hell. Where is everybody?"

This is my eternal song of complaint, the entrepreneur's favorite oratorio.

An hour later, the phone rings. An agent tells me she's got a woman celebrating her sixty- fifth birthday who wants to book twenty rooms for her family at Camp Smorgasbord! Suddenly, from zero people I've jumped to an almost full weekend! Is that a miracle or not? Isn't God looking out for me? Such miracles have happened in the past. When I crawl into the valley of despair, give up all hope, all possibility anything will ever get better, then and only then does a hand come down from heaven and lift me up. Is this the yad chazak shel Elohim I've read about in the Bible? Why do such things happen at precisely these moments? Are they accidents, or predestined events taking place only after I have "learned my lesson"?

If these metaphysical ideas are true, and I believe they are, then not only does God work actively in the world as a moral, corrective, and teaching force, but helps me in business, too.

God may be the answer to my sales problem.

Whenever I despair, Bernice tells me to go out there and sell harder, start calling people, writing letters, in other words, do something about it!

This so-called "reasonable approach" makes me want to vomit. Truth is, the worse things get, the less I do. I can't stand being bullied by people or by events. I refuse to be pushed around by my miserable business situation. So instead of doing the "reasonable thing," fighting back by trying harder, I rebel by refusing to fight. I retreat into my corner, shouting, "Fuck you!" at the rejecting world. This may not be productive, but it makes me feel better. It's as if someone stamps on my toe, and, instead of kicking them, I stamp on my other toe instead.

But perhaps instinctively I know that fighting back when you're feeling hopeless is not the answer. Waiting it out is better. I'm not in control of who registers. Only God is. It is up to Him. Why should I scream, fight, and kick? That's silly, egotistical, and fruitless. Why work so hard? Better to give in. God is stronger, more willing, and he's got all the destiny cards. I'll try here and there for the fun and sport of it, but I won't expect anything from my efforts.

As I reflect on all this, I see the answer to my sales problems: I've been doing things ass backwards. I have not followed my basic belief, which is: I shouldn't be doing sales in the first place. At first I thought I should hire others to do it. Now I understand the real answer is to wait and let God do the work for me, or rather, through me! I am the instrument. An instrument does not talk back, fight its player, or decide what notes to play. Nor does it decide to look for work. It only waits;

without its player, it is powerless, it is nothing.

I will wait for my player to decide what tune He wants to play on me. Meanwhile, I can have breakfast.

Business has a spiritual quality. It is based on the faith that God will send you customers. A phone call, a registration check in the mail, is a miracle.

When people ask, "What is your sales technique?" my answer is: prayer. I kneel before my phone and pray it will ring, kneel before my mail box and pray it will fill with registration checks.

Praying for customers is the bottom-line sales method. All else is commentary.

Losing Nutmeg

Ralph called me this morning. "You bastard!" he roared. "You guys are through up here!" We lost our Nutmeg folk dance room because I put rosin on the floor.

I am overcome by such a mixture of guilt, anger, sadness, and helplessness; I feel weak and weepy and generally kicked beyond recognition. I'm right, and they're telling me I'm wrong. I'm right, and they "fire" me.

I can't wait around for justice to be done. I've got to take action now; it's the best antidote to rage and frustration. The more I think about it, the madder I get. I've called Ralph, told him we would clean the floor ourselves or pay for a professional cleaner. His answer: "Fuck you! You guys are out!" He's not a touchy-feely kind of guy and probably has never been in therapy. Floor therapy would help him, or rosin therapy ground into his brain by hundreds of dancing feet. I'm calling Mrs. Conway. Maybe I can get to Ralph through her, or maybe there is a higher authority, like a board of directors. I may sue them for breach of contract.

Of course, we have no contract. Neither do they. We have a verbal agreement to dance until June 3. I'll ask them to honor that. Are they honorable people, or simply bastards?

Nutmeg Drifting Towards Oblivion

Imagine, the Nutmegers think I'm at fault, that I lost the room because I put rosin on the floor. I did it to protect them. Well, fuck 'em all. But I think, after the rubble clears, even Mike will see things from my point of view, namely, quality dancing on a safe floor.

In any case, the best approach for me today will be to assume that I've lost my Nutmeg group for May or forever. If they're disgusted with me because I'm fighting for quality dancing on a safe floor, then fuck them, too. (There's a lot of fucking going on here this morning, and, I'm happy to say, most of it is being done by me. Even Bernice is against me. Imagine comparing putting rosin on a dance floor to the Los Angeles riots.)

I know I'm right, even though I lost the room, even if no one agrees with me.

How nice it is to shout from the hilltops, scream from the mountains, thunder to the world at large: I am right, you fuckers! You can all go to hell as far as I'm concerned. You can do it, and I'll still be right. When you're buried underneath burning coals, I'll be on the mountain top, looking over green fields warmed by the shining sun. I'll be smiling in my personal heaven because, even though no one else agrees, I know I'm right.

It is a balm, blessing, and strengthening to stand up for your beliefs. I could lose mucho income, many folk dance "friends," the "respect" of my so-called peers. It's nice to be loved by others; but best is loving yourself. The cheese may stand alone, but it smells just fine.

The words are flowing: Anger and indignation dissipate thr-ough my finger tips. Doubt, guilt, and fear prison with all its jailers is drifting away, slowly drowning in my boiling sea. It feels great!

I'd love to strangle the disgusting creeps who are making my life miserable. I'm mowing them down with my Verbogun, freeing myself to walk down the sunny road towards my next goal.

Regarding Nutmeg: I called Mike yesterday. He hung up on me. Ridiculous. But what can I do. I called Eunice and Pete and left a message on their tape. Then I called Sam. A sane voice at last! He said the teaching was good, classes were good, and just because we lost our room was no reason not to continue classes. He said the Nutmegers would have a meeting to talk about the future.

I hung up feeling good and somewhat vindicated, and wrote Mike a letter telling him how I understood his pain and that, in spite of this problem, I had always liked working with him.

A good letter, from the heart, and without malice. In my mind, the Nutmeg incident is over. I am free, ready to move on.

Vomiting My Way to Cranbury Chapel: Back Road to the Gods, or, Beneath My Surface Lurks the Fighter

This morning's breakfast makes me nauseous, or at least writing after it does. This may be a nauseating day.

But let's not knock nausea. It may be the back road to the gods. Nausea is a weapon: You have to fight with it; you have to fight against it. Keep the flow of words coming. Don't let revulsion overcome you.

Nausea is giving me the energy to throw up this morning. I'm vomiting over the Cranbury Chapel. I fantasize a great sea of vomit engulfing that miserable place. I'd like to see Ralph Bates drown in that sea of vomit. If that can't be done, I'll settle for his burial under Puke Mountain.

I can visualize the soft greenish liquid forming in my belly, slowly mounting through my esophagus, then spurting forth with a joyous rush through both my mouth and nasal cavities and covering the living room rug of Ralph Bates's home with all kinds of artistic and folk-dance vomiting patterns.

This kind of talk is absolutely disgusting. The more I talk about vomit, the more vomititious I feel. How can I, a full-grown, moral man, an educated and polite citizen of this country with a college degree, so demean myself by wishing such foul repercussions upon an old man? Where is my sense of proportion and understanding? Truth is, I've given it all up.

We're meeting the Cranbury governing committee of the Chapel tonight. I'm hoping we can sway them to our point of view. I'm so fucking furious with these creeps! I can't get the thought of being thrown out of Cranbury Chapel on a technicality, a miserable Ralph whim, out of my head. Why are they bothering me? Why can't I just be an artist and say fuck you to everyone else?

Evidently I can't. When I want something, especially when it's important and I feel I'm justified, I simply won't accept no for an answer. I don't know where this never-give-up voice comes from. It's almost unearthly in its quality. I experienced it in Leningrad when I kept coming back to the box office day after day, sometimes twice a day, to get tickets for my tour group to see the Moldavian State Folk Dancers. I finally got them. A memorable performance! But when the ticket office refused me, I could have given up. Instead, I got more determined. I kept thinking, maybe there's another way, a better way. Every time I was about to give up, a new idea would appear. Where did these new ideas come from? It just didn't feel like me. Yet it was.

Beneath my calm, friendly, playful surface lurks a fighter. How else could I have survived as an artist? I find it very difficult to give up. In the face of resistence, I get unbelievably stubborn. Is it healthy? What about flexibility?

Whatever it is, that's the way I am. I am proud of this inner strength but hesitate to admit it. I'm proud of my stubbornness, that I won't give in, that I will resist. It is either stupid, courageous, or both. Luckily, I thrive on paradox.

Trinity

Rabbi Schneerson said, "All souls are the same; only each one has a different mission on earth." I like that. It gives meaning to the work people do: the missions of taxi driver, professor, teacher, gardener, house wife, and butcher.

But is a mission only a job? Or is there a higher purpose? Isn't the higher purpose of a taxi driver to serve people by transporting them? Isn't it the mission of teachers to transport their students to a higher plane? What is mine? Is it to write, play guitar, teach folk danc-ing, run tours, create folk dance weekends? Or does it too have a higher purpose? Is it to serve people through whatever skills I have? Intellectually, I believe so; but emotionally, I still haven't caught up to the idea. I am not certain why I do what I do. I enjoy my work, and sometimes it gives me a transcendent glow. But these "purposes" are shrouded in the relationship between me and Me. What about others? Where do they fit in?

Maybe the world is tripartite. Trinity rules. It includes me, Me, and others; it includes self, God, and service.

Take any one of these alone, and they feel meaningless.

Self alone, ego alone, me alone, isolates me from the world force.

Without little me, micro me, who will care about the big Me, God alone? Who will know Him? God wants man as instrument to ac-complish His purpose; otherwise, no one can hear His song.

I'll go for the trinity.

The Folk Dance Martyrdom of St. James

Folk dance masochism. Let's take the Cranbury Chapel incident. Mike thinks it's my fault. Whether I can convince him to be on my side or not, I don't know. I'll have to assume he's bad-mouthing me to the other Nutmeg dancers, and that my name will be mud in the Connect-icut folk dance world.

What can I do about this? The first approach would be to explain and defend my position to the Nutmeg dancers. This might help, it might not. It will cost me money in phone calls and time.

The second approach is to simply do nothing. That's what I'll do. Why bother defending myself when I know I'm right? If one of the Nutmegers is interested in my position, naturally I will explain it. But I won't go out of my way. Mike will think or say what he wants no matter what I do. So will the others.

I have no control over having my good name dragged through the mud. But I do have control over my attitude towards it. Why not adopt a positive attitude? Why not look for the pleasures of being attacked, slandered, and vilified? Why not look at the positives of folk dance martyrdom?

Consider Leopold von Sacher-Masoch, the 19th-century Austrian writer who gave masochism its name.

His sexual pleasure came from being dominated, mistreated, abused, and generally getting the shit kicked out of him. True, you often need a sadist to help you achieve these masochistic pleasures, but I'm sure we can find a few among the Nutmeg dancers. They are the ones who will love blaming me for losing Cranbury Chapel. Why should I take away their pleasure?

Why not enjoy the sting of their verbal whips as any good masochist would? Seems like a good idea, especially since my goal is to enjoy life.

If you like masochism, you'll love martyrdom. It puts you on a higher plane.

If I become a folk dance martyr, I could learn to take abuse and actually like it! Paradoxically, it would probably kill most criticism and abuse of me. After all, what pleasure can a sadist get when the victim enjoys the punishment? Any self-respecting one would soon give up in disgust. But until the sadist realizes this paradox, the masochist can get quite a bit of pleasure at no added expense. This is a revolutionary approach to abuse. I'm surprised I didn't think of it before. My creativity has been stimulated. This is why you should thank your tormentors. They are doing you a favor.

But you cannot consciously search for abuse. It has to come to you almost as a gift, by accident, via serendipity. Only then can you receive the true benefits of its paradoxical, positive-and-negative energies.

After I Write, I Go out and Fight

What does this phrase mean?

It came to me on the folk dance floor Monday night. I had a bout of depression caused by the usual questions: Why have I had eight cancellations for my Klezmer weekend in the last three days? Why are there no registrants for the Turkish tour? Why are there so few registrants for the July 4th Weekend? Should I cancel my Turkish tour? Should I cancel my July 4th Weekend? Where the fuck are the people? Where are their checks? Nothing new there.

Here's what I think: I've decided to write two hours a day, a formidable, very intense dedication. After I am finished, I need a violent break. I can run, or I can do push-ups. Both are good. Squats can be good too, especially if I do many of them.

I want to give the art of writing my best shot. What do I afterwards to release those pent-up energies?

Fight.

Let's use the Cranbury Chapel incident as a guide. Look how I fought for it. When I failed to get the room, I walked away angry and disappointed, but without regret. I'd given it my best.

Can't I apply the fighting spirit to my tours, weekends, and folk dance classes? If I battled as hard for customers as I did for the Cranbury Chapel, I might end up with more of them.

I do not want to stay depressed. I want positive, useful, expansive, wahoooo!-producing light. When I fight, I am not depressed. Even if no customers come my way, the very fact that I have put up a fight frees me. In fact, I often end up feeling elated, even though not one has registered or even shown any interest. Rather than collapsing like a wormy wimp, I have gone down fighting. There is something in that. How can you feel depressed when you are covered with personal pride and glory?

Fighting is the route I have to go. There is no choice.

Write! Then go out and fight. There is no other way.

One of the joys of leadership is that, no matter what you do or how hard you try, people still have the opportunity to hate you.

Why Write Today?

Why write today? Guilt and fear.

If I don't today, it will be easier not to tomorrow, and even easier not to the day after. Soon I'd be giving up writing completely. Better to scribble a few words than do nothing.

What about self-esteem? Does it matter? Can it prod me to pro-duce the way guilt and fear can? I doubt it. A piss on self-esteem. Guilt and fear put you on the razor's edge, kick you in the pants, attack sloth, force you to fight. The result is either a glorious win or crushing defeat.

I'm reading In Search of Ali Mahmoud, by Vivian Gornick. I al-ways liked her, even when she told me she'd found a rat in her toilet in Greenwich Village. She had a certain unapproachability, too. Now I see the untouchable part of her was her nascent writing mind. I knew her when she was a student at City College. I once visited her apart-ment in the Bronx where her mother lived. Uneventful but comfort-able: Being with Vivian was often like that. What a surprise when I first read her articles in the Village Voice. Words and characters leaped from her pages. What a writer! This was a side of Vivian I'd never known. I became her fan immediately.

A wave of depression has settled over me. I haven't felt this bad for a long time. What is it?

I relate it to the collapse of my Bulgarian and Turkish tours along with the loss of my Nutmeg folk dance group. My Bulgarian tour was cancelled because I only got two people. Not enough for me to go. I called them, told them I could put them on another tour to the Valley of the Roses, but they only wanted to travel with me. Since I wasn't going, they cancelled. I only lose money with such flattery. Now comes Turkey. Not one person registered for Turkey. Astonishing. I know business can die, but I didn't think it could die so suddenly and dra-matically. The tour business is fragile. Still, to collapse so fast, especially after the incredible success of my Budapest/Prague tour. . . .

Now I have to think about reorienting myself and set some new summer goals.

Miserable Martha

"Why can't you get more people?" Martha complained. "I shouldn't open the hotel with so few people. It doesn't pay." She made me feel guilty because I'd brought up only twenty- seven participants. How can I protect myself from the barbs of the miserable Marthas who blame me for their unhappiness? If it really didn't pay, she should have cancelled. But no, she chose to take a chance, hoping, like me, that more people would register. Is she losing money with so few? I doubt it, but I don't know.

Turkish Slide Show

This afternoon at Solway's, Joyce Dalton gave a slide show on Turkey.

Could I give one? Should I?

It would be a practical way to sell my tours. But just because it's practical doesn't mean I'll do it. Practical may be a reason for me not to do it. I need something beyond practicality to motivate me.

What pluses are there besides financial? First of all, I like to talk. A slide show is a perfect venue to talk about history, my tour experiences, geography, the frustrations of running a tour, folklore, and folk dances—a perfect set up to talk about what I like.

What else?

In order to have a slide show I need—guess what?—slides. I would have to buy and learn how to operate a slide projector. More important: I would have to take slides. That means using a camera. I've never taken photographs before. I even pride myself on never taking photographs.

Am I spreading myself too thin?

On the other hand, maybe I'm ready for a new adventure.

Preordained

I feel bad this morning. Last night I got a few calls from potential July 4th Weekenders. One idiot woman wanted to know if the $297 for three in a room covered all four days per person or per room. In other words, was that the total charge for three in a room or the charge for each person individually. It's hard to believe there are such idiots, but it's true. She actually believed I could charge about $35 per day and include three meals, all dance classes, a fine hotel, etc. Well, believe it or not, after she found out the "real" price, she cancelled. Then a couple of other people called, and I ended up with three cancellations—this for a weekend that only has nine people registered to begin with. It just about killed the project, which is half dead anyway. At this point, short of a registration miracle, the July 4th Weekend will die, too.

What am I to make of all this? Sure it's depressing to see my business slide downhill. But what can I do? Probably nothing. My former response to business reversals was to worry. But that almost never made me work harder. I'd retreat, give up, and take cover under a "fuck 'em all" attitude.

But I'm rethinking my business reversals. I've had so many it's hard to take them as seriously as I used to. After all, if I look at the bigger picture I will see that, although this year's tour to Turkey will be cancelled, I did have my most successful Budapest Prague tour to offset it. Also, although the July 4th Weekend will most likely be cancelled, I do have the luck of a Smorgasbord family registration of, they say, twenty rooms. So, on balance, I'm about even.

But I did mention business successes as gifts from heaven. If they are, how about losses? Are they, too? Or, if not gilded with the positive word "gifts," are they at least "given" from heaven? No doubt. Thus, all that it happening to me, all my successes and losses, are preordained. So are the other events in my life.

What about free choice? Do higher forces allow me the illusion of free will but actually know in advance what choices I will make? No doubt. If my business losses have been preordained, why should I worry about them? My desire to sell more tours, weekends, and folk dance classes have all have been preordained. Even my energy cycles have been preordained.

If I believe this, why should I waste my energy worrying? Preordination is a serene philosophy. Results are not up to me. I have little control over whether I'll wake up tomorrow or my plans for next week, month, or even tonight will ever materialize. It is an illusion to think I can control my destiny. Sure, I make a few small decisions—or at least it appears that way. Maybe that too is an illusion. If God knows all, then He knows what I'm thinking and doing, my future and my past, my birthday and death day. He knows when I'll have business success and failure. He also creates my worries, no doubt, to teach me about the nature of ultimate power and control.

Stretching

I have been stretching for years. It is part of my daily routine, part of my life. I've forgotten that, once upon a time, I knew nothing about it, or yoga, or running, or exercising. But today I take them for granted.

Am I cheating people by not showing them my exercises?

I love my stretch routines.

They make me feel great! Why shouldn't my folk dance students learn to stretch and get the same benefits?

But how would I teach them? I can't take time away from the dance class. On the other hand, these stretches are a necessary part of the dance class. Somehow I must introduce them to the class.

Maybe we could warm-down to classical music.

Or should I use the music of silence?

They can carry silence within them wherever they go. Why bother with external sounds when they can gain access to the music of the spheres?

Passion Smart

I believe in passion smart.

Passion is the source of motivation.

What does this have to do with giving up my Monday night folk dance group? I have to replace it with something. First, I would replace it with a vacuum. What I like about a Monday night vacuum is, it makes me nervous. An idea is cooking. No idea is worthy unless it starts to make me nervous.

David's call promoted these thoughts. I had hoped to take the summer off, especially those two August weeks when all my work would stop and I could devote myself completely, day and night, to uninterrupted writing, guitar practice, and running. Those weeks were to be the centerpiece of my summer experiment. Then David called. He said the family wanted to come to visit exactly during that precious, experimental time! What a downer. Instead of concentrated peace, of devotion to writing and guitar, I would have concentrated kids running around the house, unmitigated quasi-chaos, noise, and no concentration. Basically, it would totally ruin my summer. But how could I say that to my own kids?

Then I thought, God is sending a message through my children. David's coming has "pushed the envelope." It's made me realize how important this experiment really is to me, how important to keep writing and keep practicing. I don't just want to do it for two weeks in August but for the rest of my life! I have to thank David for this realization. It's also a reason for giving up Monday night.

I'm also thankful for the cancellation of my August Turkish tour. It has given me time to rethink my priorities, to dedicate myself to a summer of writing and guitar practice. Leading tours has given me the confidence to choreograph, improvise, and be a strong leader. I've learned that becoming the president of Jim Gold International, a large corporation with many tours going to different countries, led by members of my staff, is not for me.

That is why I lost my Turkish tour this summer. It was a signal from the higher power to rethink my direction.

Never Again!

When I got home from teaching folk dancing at the JCC, two of my expectations collapsed. First, the promised twenty-room registration of the Family Steingart fell through. She didn't get one family member to join her! Not one! What a creep she must be. Of course, I care, not about her creephood, but only about all the money I will lose on that weekend. If she had filled twenty rooms, that would have been about forty people and I would have made about $4,000. That is mucho money, especially when you consider that the Turkish tour collapsed this summer, and that I have no other work for August. Four grand would have put me through August. . . .

These financial collapses have been sent to test my writing-guitar-running happiness program. Does it really work? If not I'll have to start worrying about money again.

Never! Never again! I will not go on that miserable dowhill route! I'm sick of the worry road. It's either forward or death! I shall not regurgitate those old tired worn-out ways across the fresh clean carpet of the present.

Expectations

This morning I read the obituaries in the New York Times. Many of the subjects were my age or close to it. When it's time for me to move on, will my death be depressing? Or will it be a form of relaxation?

These thoughts really began with the death of the Steinhart Family Reunion at Camp Smorgasbord this summer. The booking of those twenty rooms died very quickly. So did my $4,000 profit. I had even factored the profit into my summer finances, and, bang, lost it all in one deathly moment.

I had built up my expectations until I believed my expectations were part of reality. The excitement of a potential $4,000 profit soon built into the expectation of a $4,000 profit and then the acceptance of a $4,000 profit. All this before it even existed. My "profit" was only a dream.

The question is: how to live longer and expect less. Better yet: how to live longer and expect nothing. Best of all would be: forget about living longer altogether—it is merely another expectation. Rather, live without expectations.

Hard to do. That's a high art form, the pinnacle of the art of life. Expecting nothing would fill my days with quiet joy and meditation.

Imagine reading the stock pages and expecting nothing. It is almost impossible to conceive. Don't I invest in stocks to see them go up? My future pleasure would be destroyed by lack of expectations. But I would also be wiping out future pain when my stocks go down. I would be living on an even keel, a new and strange phenomenon.

Wisdom flows when I contemplate death.

The Smorgasbord Steinhart family cancellation is a metaphor for the pain of expectation. So is my love of New Valley Corporation stock. That stock has gone from one cent to forty. I bought 4,000 shares about two years ago at about forty cents. At that time it was Western Union. After I purchased it, the company almost went bankrupt. My stock went down to one cent and it stayed at one for about two years. Then, in bankruptcy court, after changing the name to New Valley Corporation and divesting itself of most of its business, it actually began making money on the Western Union-name moneygrams. About a month ago, First Data corporation made an offer to buy the bankrupt company.

The offer was refused, but the stock suddenly jumped to twelve cents. I had lunch with Charlie Erickson, who used to work for Western Union. He said friends told him the company was doing okay. After talking to him, I decided to take a chance, called Joel, and told him to buy $1,000 worth of stock. We ended up getting 10,000 shares at twelve cents. Two weeks ago, another company made a higher offer for New Valley Corporation. The stock went up again. Now it's at forty cents. I'm even on my original 4,000 shares and ahead on my newly purchased 10,000.

My expectations built. First, I imagined the stock at one dollar and a quick profit of $10,000. Then I thought, Why stop at a dollar? After all, the stock could go to five, to ten, even to fifty. I'll be a millionaire! And this in only twenty seconds of imagining! Soon my hopes for a reasonable profit escalated into life changing financial glory. I was setting myself up for a quick expectation slide.

Sure enough, when I called Joel yesterday, he said the stock had fallen to six cents! Turned out his computer had made a mistake, and it was still trading at forty; nevertheless, for an hour I had to look for my heart in my feet.

So much for the ups and downs of the market, the roller coaster ride of expectations.

On Marketing: What is Enough?

I am taking off this summer to write and practice guitar. This is the product development phase of my business. I am developing stories, books, articles, and a new guitar concert program. I am running my own personal R and D department.

Once my products are developed, I'll market them. Marketing means convincing others your products are worthy of purchase. But why should I have to convince anyone?

I am, on the other hand, weak in marketing. I will do almost anything to avoid it.

Yet perhaps I am already marketing to the best of my ability but don't realize it. After all, I have been making a living for years in a practically impossible field. I must be doing something right, even though I am doing what I believe to be the absolute sales minimum. Wouldn't it be strange to find out that I have been selling my products at full capacity ever since I started?

The truth is, in spite of my so-called hatred of sales, I am a good salesman.

I am selling the best I can and the best I need to. I don't need great wealth or a large following, just enough to get along and support my artistic habits.

Why do I want freedom in the first place? Primarily to follow the unknown road of art adventure and explore the mystery beyond.

Attitude

Why push for excellence if ultimately we are all forgotten? Why not just lie down and die? Is it immoral? I thought about this as I was driving along Route 17 on my way to my July 4th Weekend at the Paramount Hotel. These are not questions of purpose or meaning. They are questions of attitude.

The world is built on attitudes. Purpose comes afterwards; so does meaning. Attitude is the prime ingredient of creation. When God created the world He had a positive attitude.

INVENTIONS

Leif Ericsson Meets Lord Berserk

Leif Ericsson takes his adventure across the fiords, over the green mountains padded with growling grass and poison trees reaching out, touching him, torching him with belly- belching fire from the center of the earth.

Leif is unafraid. He trudges among foot bandages and gnarled knee trunks bent at the hip, plopping and piercing, foot after foot, on his unknown way to America. Discoveries are never easy, but what choice is there? Morning sandwiches have not yet arrived. Drinking coffee and eating doughnuts in an American restaurant is no mean feat, especially with the eleventh century watching.

These are stories coated with the wax of ancient times. Vikings peruse a dark hall laden with Byzantine silks and images of pristine Druidic hordes from the Celtic East, where Tartar- running is the mode. Don't stretch too much, else the break comes.

Leif has no friends. Who else is as crazy as he? How can he relate to the mere sanity of these dullards and unadventurous louts living around him? To strike out across lonely, dangerous seas for unknown lands fraught with danger and hard beauty—that is the beatific life of a crazy man.

Leif kneels before his master, Lord Berserk. Dressed in bear skins and with traces of shaving cream still dripping from his beard, the nobleman crowns the bare head of his first and only subject. He declares in a deep fiordian voice: "Oh, Leif, sail on. Let no nascent whale or bloated walrus dent your enthusiasm for the insane; let no lackey of dripping blues besmirch your belly-busting visions. You will conquer the world, my lad, and your tools will be blindness and foolishness. Let the dried-up hags of village politics vent their empty rages upon you; let the empty-nested, brain-barren creators of thatched-roof philosophies rail against you. These mean nothing when a man is on the permanent search for the spirit gold. And indeed, my Leif, you shall find it far away beyond the dark field of seas. Therefore, my son, I give you my bear blessing. Go forth and conquer the black waves of fear, beat the wind with your iron fist, and create a new world on the fir tree ashes of the old."

"Thank you, Master Berserk," said Leif. "I am sinking into a murky dream. The camouflage beyond the tree tops makes no sense. I will conquer the road beyond lands, reach for the path beyond stars. Bless me with your bearskin tunic. My journey shall be long and endless, and only burning love and fiery attachments shall carry me to the edge."

GOD

Fear of God

I've given up. That may be the beginning of something new or the end of something old. I've given up on worrying about money. Let God handle it. God is the one who makes my stocks go up or down, who sends me bookings, registrations, and customers, who fills my folk dance classes or makes them small. God runs the show. Why should I fight Him? What can I do against Him, anyway? I might as well work with Him, accept his rule and decisions. I'm wasting my time worrying about money. What good has it done me? What has it brought me? Does worrying about money get customers to call me? No. Does it get people to register for my tours, or dancers to come to class? No. Does it get me bookings or make my stocks go up? No. It's useless mental masturbation—as if my worry would force others to do something about it, as if others even cared about my worry. Not only do they not, they don't even know about it. And if they knew, they wouldn't care anyway. Why should they? Worry is my show. Let God worry. I'm going on vacation.

But God won't worry. It's not His nature. Instead, He will do what he wants in His own good time while I lie on the beach waiting for directions.

Now I can see why I have no energy, why I'm so down. I've got nothing to worry about. Without that, I have no motivation. Worry has been my prime mover for years. Take it away, and I'm lost. How can I live without it? What will push me? Worry has given power to both my right and left leg. I need fear to walk. This all raises a good question: Is life empty without fear? Should man fear? Or should he live a life free of worry? Which is better?

I am now worry-free. But am I happier? No. I'm miserable. I wish I could find a worry to motivate me. I hate this blugh, insipid, enervated state.

I just read a line that says Jews should fear only God. Maybe I should transfer my fears to God. If I did, that would mean I believe in His power to take care of me. It's a two-way street, after all: I fear Him, do what he says; He in turn takes care of me. Not a bad deal. This way I could instill fear in myself and get back some energy.

But, as I say, part of the deal is to do what He wants. What's that? What does He expect from me? If he's going to send me bookings, money, luck, customers, health, security, and all the other worry-free goodies, what must I do for Him? Does He have any rules He wants me to follow? Should I send Him a present on His birthday? I read that God wants Jews to study Torah and perform the 613 mitzvahs. That's a lot of mitzvahs. I don't even know what most of them are. Should I look them up or sit around and wait for His personal directions to me? Probably the latter. God put artistic talents in my hands. How and where should I use them? Does He want me to give concerts, teach folk dancing, run weekends, lead tours? Does He want me to run, do yoga, study and learn languages? If this is the case, I'll just keep doing what I'm doing.

Perhaps God wants me to worship Him and not to waste my time worrying. If that is true, how should I? Through my art? He gave me talent for a reason. I must develop it. God might say, use it for the benefit of others to improve the world. After all, tikkun is coming, the Messiah is coming, the Resurrection is coming, and eventually the world will be one and there will be universal peace. At that time, people may live forever—using replaceable parts, of course. Anyway, this is all far in the future. For now I still have to answer the question of how to fear God constructively, how to use my talents is the service of something bigger than my miserable money-worrying ego.

Suppose I fear God and no one else. Suppose He has given me a mission, and that mission is to develop my talents to the fullest and, in the process, serve others.

In other words, I'd better damn well fulfill my mission; otherwise God will punish me. I like that. It scares me. Thank God for that. I'm alive again. I've touched something I believe in. There's no question that, when I don't bring my skills to the world, I feel sick, wasted, and useless. If I don't do what I consider to be right, I usually end up vomiting. Suppose God thinks this is right for me. This was the mission He gave me to perform. It is my duty. The 613 mitzvahs are contained somewhere in this duty. When I do what I'm supposed to, the mitzvahs suffuse my being and I feel wonderful. When I back off, am lazy, give in to my lower desires, I end up feeling ashamed and wasted, a useless stick tossed and floating aimlessly on the ocean.

I often wake up in the morning afraid I won't fulfill my task. I usually deny this fear. How can I face such awesome responsibility so early in the morning?

But my fear is there. Is it my form of awe, my fear of God?

Yes, it is.

Resurrection

I have put too much trust in straight lines, not enough in curves, dotted lines, and dashes. The path to heaven rarely goes straight up.

Sometimes you must take side roads, zigzagging byways; sometimes you ascend hills leading nowhere or ride into valleys covered with fog, lined with dirty rocks and barren tree stumps, all in an attempt touch the heavenly spark. Perhaps that is why I begin so many mornings depressed. I'm starting out stuck in a black pit of tar in a hidden valley, surrounded by fires, pots of boiling lead, and steaming water. Every day I fight to escape; every day it is the same struggle. Perhaps I am bored with myself, tired of routines and of thinking the same thoughts. Perhaps those thoughts have lost their luster: Each day I must rediscover their shine.

Truth is a shining, amorphous, blazing mass of infinity, an untouchable ball of timeless particles, an unheard gong ringing throughout the universe. There is no way to permanently capture its essence. Yet each day I strive to reach it.

Yesterday I had a handle on truth, felt it pulsate through the living dance, music, song, writing, running, yoga, and reading. I was alive and awake! But during the night I lost touch with the celestial fire. In the morning I awoke, a dolt in pajamas, mumbling, grumbling, and stumbling around the living room, searching for my morning coffee to put me back in touch with yesterday's sparks, those blazing deities who led me so well. They are no longer available. God died during the night. I have to resurrect Him every morning.

I am a reflection of the sun and its movement. I rise in the morning, sluggish and sleepy, and drink in the light. I work to recapture the spark of that fireball eternally passing above me. I worship the sun, whose greatness lies deep within me. Every day my search begins anew.

Hidden and amorphous, the living fire dwells in a tent somewhere north of my liver.

Peace of Mind

A wonderful interview with Sadat in Gail Sheehy's book Pathfinders, and a beautiful example of Islamic fatalism. Sadat says, "Let me tell you, I am a true believer. I believe every human being has a mission to fulfill and a time to live. I start with what we call in the military 'appreciation of the situation.' What's my duty now? And then, once I make my decision, I put myself in the hands of God. Whatever happens, I am happy. Succeed or die, I have done my best."

Sheehy then asks Sadat, "What is your personal attitude towards death?"

"I don't fear it at all," he replies. "The Koran tells us it is God who has fixed this hour, and He has fixed it already for you. . . . God has put it. So I am at ease. Great ease."

I love it: Fatalism brings peace of mind. You can do your best, too.

Tikkun Olam and Business

Tikkun olam, Judaism's spiritual mandate to repair the world, is an excellent mandate for business.

Beyond money and egoism, tikkun olam unifies writing, music, folk dancing, tours, and weekends. Its higher purpose unites business ventures with artistic ventures.

It leads to self-fulfillment in my land of crazy brains running wild. I'll repair the world and myself in the process. What could be better?

July-September 1994

WRITING

Study of Myself

Looking back, it seems that Handfuls of Air and Mad Shoes were my best work. I love reading them, especially the latter. Others have not had that reaction. In fact, the stupendous silence on publication of Mad Shoes truly amazed me. I believe it is a wonderful book. Why couldn't others recognize it? I love the character of Sylvan, the characters of Sam Ferdinand, Dr. Lume, and Schlossberger. Why didn't others? Well, some did, but few.

But my New Leaf Journal is different. It wasn't written for public readings but for private exploration. It is my personal workbook, my way of working things out in my head and, in so doing, putting them out of my head. I'm just thinking out loud. No preconceived order or form. Only the pour-out-the-words 'method.' Is anyone else interested in knowing me? Who knows?

But why should I tell anybody about this? Why bother explaining my secret of how self- improvement drives me forward? If this journal is written for me, why 'share' it with anybody? (Of course, if someone reads over my shoulder or asks, I wouldn't hesitate to give it to them.)

It's so easy to write pages and pages of I, I, I. I can talk about I, I, I almost without stop.

Deep in my heart I would love someone to be interested enough in me, me, me to read it, to be fascinated with the inner workings of my mind because I love my mind and I love myself and I love everything about myself, even the miserable parts, and I would love all my parts to be recognized and have an effect on someone besides myself. I have a yearning to be effective, to reach out and change the world, a messianic inner fervor that I hesitate to admit. But admit it I must. It only comes out in my writing. That's why this study of myself is so important to me.

How can I admit this love to others? It is so egotistical and self-centered. I would like to think of them, help them, be other-directed; but my mind doesn't work that way.

Birth of the Personal Therapy Writing Program

Ginny called yesterday to say what wonderful tours we went on. "Remember Hungary? Remember the Soviet Union, Egypt, Israel?" Yes, I remember them. Those tours were among the highlights of my life.

I woke up this morning with a yen for self-improvement. Somehow I feel stuck. I have no future projects, no upcoming adventures. I'm working in the field of the known. It's not bad, but it doesn't thrill and excite like the unknown.

It's a quiet time. I'm becoming a sage. It is quite boring.

Perhaps there are no great adventures without great fears, no great excitement without great worry. When my tour business began, I searched for customers, took language lessons, studied history, centered my year around the upcoming country I would tour. Now I know the countries; the adventure is gone. Even new places like Sweden, Norway, and Denmark somehow seem like more of the same with a slight twist. I've got to move on to something else.

What?

Some of my downs come from reading this journal. Starting in January with my four-pages- a-day writing commitment, I thought I was on to new and exciting adventure. Barry and my writing class liked much of my "new" material. Now I'm reading New Leaf again. It's okay, but nothing sensational, nothing I even want to read in public.

I am considering a return to performing. But it is a return to something old, hopefully on a higher level. I am a seasoned concert veteran. Part of this means I am calmer and more skeptical about bookings. The thrill of beginning a new career is gone. So are the fears. I am calmed, cured of them, and slightly depressed: Who wants to be cured, anyway? Isn't it better to have a dream, and an impossible one at that? But what can I do? That's the state I am in. I can only ride the waves and wait for something to turn up on the horizon.

Words about my life and feelings flow. Writing has become my therapy. I talk to my computer.

Who wants to read that? Therapists? Patients? Others?

Though this journal is helpful to me, me, me, maybe it can offer others the idea of writing about them, them, them—writing as cure, therapy, fulfillment, and self-exploration.

I want to offer something of value and make myself valuable in the process. Hopefully, the quality and quantity of my pages will inspire others to do the same, to see that "self-writing" is okay and an adventure in itself. You can say things to your journal that you can't say to anyone else, plus end up with a written record. You can refer to past thoughts and discover new ones in the process.

Inward, meditative, sad, adventurous and exhilarating, writing as therapy is my offering. I hope others accept it. If they don't, they are jerks.

Yesterday, reading passages from this book, I was amazed to see how good they were! I should read my own journals for my own good. They remind me how quickly I forget what is important to me and how eloquently, at times, I have tried to remind myself on paper about those higher values.

Even though I wrote those passages only a few months ago, it feels like I'm reading someone else. I'm developing some objectivity and perspective. I also realize the person writing is not only me, but someone else as well—a difficult concept to grasp. Intellectually, it is easy to understand; we are all part of the same tree. But to practice this belief, to sit down, read your own work, and feel someone else has written it, is a talent and a blessing.

Reading my work as someone else's is a major step in annihilating my ego. Perhaps I can even shorten the distance between my writing and editing. For the editor's eye is the eye of the other writer living in my brain.

Another reminder I found is the importance of daily writing. It seems for a short period during the last few months I was onto important truths about myself. I poured them into New Leaf, and the results are there, written for all to see. I want to keep the daily writing habit. But often vicissitudes blow you in contrary directions and you forget what is truly important. My journal acts as my ballast. By reading the best passages in it, I am rediscovering a self I forgot, a fundamental, building, creative self that can forge personal masterpieces.

Seeing positives in my prose, recognizing inherent powers, not being afraid of admiring my creativity, says something about the new stage of life I am in. Slowly, inexorably, I am beginning to have confidence in myself. It is moving from mini-confidence to some confidence to mucho confidence to maxi-confidence. I haven't reached maxi yet or even much of mucho, but I am on my way. I don't know why, after almost fifteen years of working with stage fright, performance anxiety, and all the other downers of the onstage life, I have suddenly come to grips with this. This probably goes with my newfound ability to read my New Leaf and believe someone else wrote it.

I never want to go back to my old destructive negative self.

I like this new me—powerful, dynamic, realistic, and calm, based on inner strength without lots of outer movement, a bedrock belief in something.

Writing

Oh Lord, thank you for the writing tool, for bestowing a gift of freedom and putting a cure in my hands. Four pages a day will lift my sorrows and anoint my sagging skin with new ointments of energy. Lord, You are guiding me again, pointing the way out of this dark, wet, dank, forlorn, and whiskey-logged hole. I'll never leave You again, I promise. You wanted me to see, feel, explore, and use the power of the Word.

My sadness is washing away, my cloud slowly lifting; the sun is peeking from behind tattered trees. You have given me the power to instill truth across the computer screen that masquerades as the mask behind my brain.

It's a shame I'm not promoting my writing. I have many pages, some quite good, sitting in my house. My books, too.

Jesus needed Paul to preach the gospel. Without Paul, Jesus would be unknown today. I need a Paul. Where is he? Will he ever appear?

Must I be my own Paul? My performing talent is just sitting here, too. So are my tours and weekends. My talents develop and develop and develop. Will I ever want to bring them to market?

Minimal marketing is my talent. In writing, no marketing is my talent. I produce abundance. Then I wait, hoping someone will magically take in my new crop. Will they? Does magic work? Maybe. After all, I am still surviving in my crazy field of work. Most people don't survive at all. That in itself is a victory.

Tomorrow night I am giving my debut performance, doing a reading for the Bergen Poets Society—another example of minimal marketing at its best. Performance is my best sales tool. I do it "naturally." Could it be that, by deciding to return to performance, I am deciding to return to sales? Are the two synonymous? I think so. I am returning to the world, giving up the dream of a monk's life. At last night's group meeting, when I asked, "Are financial fears forever?" everyone answered,

"Yes!"

Rebirth and Resurrection in the Flesh

Last night I had my first good business idea in months: start a Beginners Folk Dance Class with Registration Only on Monday night. This is the best way to teach beginners.

I've had a beginners-only folk dance class in mind for years. I've tried it for years on all my folk dance nights from 7 to 8 p.m. But when advanced dancers trickled in, beginners saw them dance and got discouraged. Most eventually dropped out. Also, I am playing the guitar with the right-wrist-deep- relaxation technique that Alexander Bellow taught me. Finally it is starting to click. It's taken almost thirty years. Could I be so dumb? Or is that the nature of art, maturation, and learning? I've been through this breakthrough-and-success syndrome many times in the past only to see it slip back to stagnation and failure. I am skeptical about this breakthrough, but I also believe it is for real. An old idea in new form.

I, too, am an old idea in new form. I am experiencing a business and guitar rebirth. Am I also experiencing a writing rebirth?

Yesterday Barry read my work and talked again about plot and structure and why James Joyce's Finnegan's Wake and Gertrude Stein's works hold together; they are readable classics even though they are incomprehensible, because they have a structure, a plot, a theme.

He mentioned Leif Erickson, and something luminous clicked in my mind. Could my New Leaf journal have a structure? A plot? A theme? Perhaps I should change the name to New Leif. Leif Erickson sailed across the Atlantic and discovered America. New Leif could be the story of New Leif Erickson, a modern Leif Erickson who discovers a new country as yet unknown to contemporary twentieth-century man. What a plot that would be!

Battleground

I'm sitting at the table in the backyard, writing in my notebook computer. I want to see what writing outside feels like.

Out here words feel more like dreams in the summer mist.

I breathe deeply, then hold my breath.

I focus, envisioning my mind floating over a warrior's field. It is the battleground where I will fight to control my wandering mind.

I can't stand Thoreau's turgid style. It's like reading a book with soup on my glasses. But when Barry gave me *The Heart of Thoreau's Journals* to read, I thought I'd give him another try. I still don't like him. Why is Thoreau so popular? What is so great about him? His importance to me is the fact that his journal was published. My New Leaf Journal may be published some day; it's worthy. If reading Thoreau's journals makes me see my worthiness, all the better. Still I'd rather read my journal than his.

Thoreau became famous after his died. Do I have to wait that long? Perhaps I ought to check out the journals of other writers. But is that necessary? After all, the question is: Can my New Leaf Journal be worthy? If I believe it is, why bother reading the journals of other writers, unless they are authors like Paul Brunton who write what I love to read.

Writing My Own Copy

I wish I wrote my own tour copy. Up to now, I have hated doing it. That's why I give it to Arlene, and she does a mediocre to fair job of it. I could do a better one, or at least I stamp it with my personality. But whenever I write my own copy, it comes out strange, crazy, and off-the-wall. Arlene thinks this will chase away customers. She may be right. That is why I haven't written my own tour brochures, publicity, and advertising. The few times when I have—for example, weekend fliers—I invented mythical guest folk dance teachers as well as other entertainers, philosophers, authors dead, alive, and not yet born, all who planned to show up on the weekend. I had lots of fun writing these fliers, and I loved showing them to others. I liked my sly creative "twists and lies." When I write my weekend programs, they have the same off-the-wall style. Some call it disguised hostility. I partly agree. Perhaps disguised hostility doesn't sell. But writing it is so much fun! And it's not all repressed anger, anyhow; some is simply my mind pouring blarney across the pages. Traditional advertising bores me. If I have to write that straight-jacketed copy, I'd rather not write at all.

And I don't; I give it to Arlene.

Suppose I said, "I'm writing my own copy whether it sells or not. I don't care what my customers think." I might lose some anyway, but I might gain some, too. Who knows? At least I'll be having fun. Why not apply the freedom of journal writing to advertising copy?

How would I do this?

First, I must be prepared to lose all my customers. Do I dare take such a chance? Am I ready to lose them? Arlene says she writes like the average person because she knows how the average person thinks. Maybe she does. But perhaps my tours and weekends are not for the average person. Generally, the average person is not interested in folk dancing. The average person is interested in bowling, movies, watching TV, and eating at McDonald's. Is this the clientele I am looking for? Would they want to learn an 11/16th Bulgarian kopanitsa, a Greek hasapikos, a Romanian bruil, or anything similar?

I am looking for unaverage people, customers who are partly off the wall, a clientele who have long ago fallen out of bed. (Naturally, I want them sane and rational enough to pay for my events.) I want customers who dance and function both on and off the beat.

On a deeper level, knowing what people want is beyond me. I can only know what I want; I can verbalize my own vision whether it be on or off-the-wall. Those who appreciate this vision will become my customers.

I should write advertising copy the way I write my journal, the way I write my stories.

I am going to start writing my own copy. I've already started. My first flier was for the new Beginner Folk Dance class. It said: Wanted: New Folk Dancers! One left foot. . . two left feet. . . three left feet. . . . This sentence has my stamp on it. My second flier for the Yoga and Folk Dance Weekend had my calligraphy in the design. Now I'm ready to go "big time." Big time means "little time." In the past, by trying to appeal to everybody (witness my acceptance of Arlene's bumper sticker Folk Dancing Is For Everyone), I was trying to reach the entire county, state, country, and world. Big mistake. I'm looking for the Bulgarian 11/16th crowd, those who worship 7/8ths and 9/16ths rhythms.

I want to like my customers. I want to love my business!

Writing and Publishing

I cringe at the thought of editing. What do other writers do, edit all their stuff? I can't imagine the day ever coming when I will go through mine. At this rate, I'll be averaging over a thousand pages a year! I'm turning out almost one New Leaf a month now, and I'm just getting warmed up. If I live forty more years, that means I'll end up with over forty thousand pages. How will I edit that? Or will it die with me? If it does, is that so bad? Sure, as my mother said, "It's a shame to give up the violin after all that practicing. All that talent and hours of work gone to waste." The same thing for my writing. Hours spent, all that talent, pages of insights, gone to waste. My writing will end up where my violin ended up. I'll end up there, too—dead, wasted, and forgotten. Maybe indifference to my fate and the fate of my creations is the best way to go. Certainly Buddha and the other sages would say so. So would many Westerners.

I'd like to feel sublime indifference to the fate of my work. But I don't. I think it is a shame my work may not be published, that it may die in my closet, that no one will read it. But what can I do? Am I fated to have no promotional talent or desire to publicize or push my work?

Well, I do have desire but am secretly too proud to give in to it. I stubbornly refuse to publish, to promote and push—a matter of personal pride. They will have to come to me.

Where did I ever get such crazy notions? Do I derive some secret good, some mysterious strength, from them?

Perhaps I know intuitively that, if my efforts go into publicizing and pushing my work, I will no longer put effort into creating them. Part of the creative process thrives on secrecy, surprise, and serendipity. I don't know where this magical process of creation will lead me. How can I ask others to follow? I'm too busy trying to find my own way through the maze I work in.

Should I put some money into hiring someone who will push my stuff for me?

On Recognition

My desire to publish is largely due to my desire for *recognition*. But I also realize the desire for recognition *robs me of my power!* Attachment to rewards is precisely what Indian philosophy warns you against. Work, but desire not the fruits of your labor. Once you start worrying about recognition, your mind goes outward, focusing on what others can do for you. You start losing focus; your inspiration, power, and vision start dribbling away. Forget, therefore, about recognition or any other fruits. Retain your power and purity. Good idea. . .but so hard to remember.

This morning I tried not to write.

Why?

When I woke up, I had nothing to say.

But I have nothing to say on most days.

In fact, almost every time I sit down to write I start out by having nothing to say. I discover what I want to say as I write.

This seems quite natural. If I already *knew* what I had to say, I wouldn't bother writing at all.

LANGUAGES

Soothing, Soothing

Relax, relax. "Relax" is a terrible English word, so counterproductive in sound. How can you relax when the end of a word assaults your senses with the crashing "x" sound?

Better to find soothing sounds to bathe your body, gentle lulling sounds to caress your ears and heart: the lovely "l's", the rolled "r's", and the soothing, soothing "n's" and "m's".

Before Babel Fell: One Language

Yesterday we were eating supper at Sid and Phoebe's when somehow we began talking about language with one of their linguist friends. My spirit rose. Language! A linguist! My forgotten lover! The hole in my soul sewed up.

What had caused the emptiness?

I easily understood. I had given up my study of Hebrew, taken it off the burner completely. In order to learn the correct pronunciation and meanings of Sanskrit words in the yoga texts, I had taken Teach Yourself Sanskrit and my Sanskrit tapes off the shelf and started studying them. I couldn't do two languages at once. Hebrew had to go.

My commitment to Sanskrit was minimal. It was not a long-range project, only a break in my chain of language study. Without my study of Hebrew I felt empty.

Evidently, I need to study languages for the rest of my life. I may always be a dilettante, but, as Sid said, that's not so bad. I don't have time to be an expert in everything.

I can't devote six hours a day to languages. Anyhow, the world may have One Language subdivided into hundreds of smaller groups. If this is true, then it really doesn't matter what language I study. They are all branches of the same tree: Hebrew, Russian, Greek, Hungarian, Czech, Arabic, Hindi, Sanskrit, Turkish, Bulgarian, Spanish, French, Italian, German, Old Norse, and more. An hour a day is a good commitment to study it.

LIFE

The Pain Shift

Work is the best way to suffer and grow. It gets the circulation going and gives me a few short stretches of joy.

Unsatisfied with the way things are, I constantly work at getting better. My puritan-ethic heart beats through almost every activity, giving it meaning and substance, and serving as a constant tool of self-torture.

During the past fifteen years, I have gone to the mountain. I have studied, practiced, trained, retreated, returned, given up, tried new approaches to free myself from the pain of performance.

The attempt has been a total failure. Pain is here to stay. I'll have to content myself with occasional sparks of joy. But even they will never come unless I dive into the striving and suffering needed to achieve excellence. The final measure is performance. It tests your skills, resourcefulness, inventiveness, and imagination, gives you a wall to climb with real measurements in the physical world.

Mr. Vladimir, my violin teacher—what a pain he was! Am I a pain when I teach? I hope so. I want my students to climb upward on the ladder of excellence.

Running tours causes pain, too. That's why I stopped running them for two years. At first, I was relieved. But I soon started missing them. I had lost my pain but also my excitement and adventure. Evidently, you can't have adventures, thrills, and pleasure without dealing with pain. So I started running tours again. Now I have both pain and pleasure— excitement with occasional clouds of depression and misery passing overhead. Life is a cyclical roller coaster ride. The only way to avoid it is to get off and die.

Out of the Closet

The days of my secret desire to become a monk have ended. I am "using" the world to measure my skills, my talents, my accomplishments. The world is both opposition and lover. I must conquer it to get my point of view across, yet, in the end, I must love it, too, since love and opposition are my partners in a perfect imperfect marriage.

I'm out of the closet, tours and all! I hope you like what I do.

But if you don't, I'm going to keep doing it for you anyway, performing and polishing until someday I hope you will love me just as someday I hope to love you.

Back Pain

For the first time in months I have a lower back pain. It started after my yoga lesson with Rama. It hit after I told him I was afraid to do certain yoga exercises because I might hurt my back. He said, "No one hurts their back in yoga. It is impossible. Yoga is done very slowly, very cautiously. As you do it, you are constantly listening to your body, monitoring it, watching it. If you feel a pain coming on, you do not push beyond it. Hold it, watch it, analyze it. In my experience as a yoga teacher no one has hurt their back doing yoga. They have hurt their back doing other things."

I said, "Yes, I'm sure if you do yoga the right way, you won't hurt your back. But I am imperfect."

That's where he disagreed with me. "You are perfect," he said. "You simply may not realize it yet."

I couldn't disagree with him. I couldn't agree with him either. I liked what he said, the possibility that, in yoga, I had found a perfecting way. Only when I have abused it by pushing the postures beyond pain have I hurt myself. His words confirmed my experience. But I had never heard anyone actually say these things. I'd read many books on yoga philosophy, so when he said it, I knew he was right. He believed it, and I did, too.

Yet ever since I left Rama, my back has been hurting.

Could it be that I want to find a teacher who knows everything, can guide me, and tell me what to do? Someone who's a model of perfection in whom I can believe and give myself up to totally? Am I looking for a god instead of a teacher? When Rama said no one hurts their back doing yoga, the old hope returned. Maybe at last I had found the final and ultimate teacher who could lead me to personal salvation. All I would have to do is listen, drink up his words, bow to his commands, and I would be redeemed.

But I no longer believe so. Teachers are merely humans with a spark of deity. Their spark may well ignite the wood within me, but the final sparks will be mine. They always have been. There is no hope at all that Rama can fulfill my ancient unrealistic wishes. So when he spoke, my disbelief in perfection clashed with my hope for it. The war between skepticism and hope took place in my lower back.

Rama reflects my power. A part of me hates to accept it. I wish I could give it to someone else. It's lonely, insecure, and frightening to be free and accept responsibility for myself. Please, please, please—I want to throw my self away, to crash on some distant shore, broken, mortified, and struggling to rise as a beneficent god stands above me, coaxing and guiding. I hate, hate, hate being all alone in the universe. I can't take the responsibility of being right. I want to be wrong, wrong, wrong, on the bottom, crawling with the worms, bowing before higher beings who control my destiny. Anything is better than standing alone on the mountain roaring with responsibility for myself. I prefer to be weak and crumbling, to merge with molecules of water in the ocean, then to evaporate, joining the invisible air particles.

The more I speak of these things, the worse my back gets. I can hardly get up. My pain is growing. . .and I know why. But I can't stop it yet. I have to follow the growth pattern, ride the waves of psychological misery, until the solution works out by itself. My back pain will dissolve when I work out my problem.

Rama cannot be my leader—even though I wish he could. No one can be my leader. Only I can be my leader.

Realizing this will cure my back pain.

When Rama said I can't hurt my back doing yoga, my faith in him fell apart. Who could make such a stupid statement? Anyone can get hurt doing yoga. Human beings are imperfect vessels. By saying this, Rama lost his god potential. I wanted a god, but got a yoga teacher. Rama's business card says "yoga teacher." There is no mention of god. He has not advertised himself as a deity. Only my expectations and hopes have created a false prophet. I am disillusioned but closer to reality. I'm looking forward to the time when I will bless my disillusionment and say good-bye to back pain.

Back Pain Continued

We're at the farm this morning, where the air is cool and fresh. The Wenokors are with us. They took our bed. We slept in Jonny and Christie's bed with its soft mattress.

I woke up with a back ache.

It is a continuation of yesterday's back ache. I was fine yesterday, fine last night. I'm awful today. I'm trying to analyze why my back hurts. I'm looking for psychological reasons. Yet finding them doesn't necessarily make my back better—not right away, at least. It takes time for knowledge to sink in. This morning I came up with the following explanations:

1. Rama complimented my yoga postures. I find it difficult to accept my new yoga self- image of competence, strength, and skill.

2. I find it difficult to accept my new self-image of writing competence, strength, and skill. As I read New Leaf I find the writing excellent. It seems like my best ever. I am coming into my own. How can I accept this? In fact, even as I started to write this paragraph, I felt a sharp pain in my lower back, the center of my resistance, which protects me by reminding me that, if I show competence, excellence and strength, Big Mama will smash me on the head. So my lower back resists the call for excellence. It is conservative, protective, not daring. It represents the weight of the past, the heavy habits of weakness and incompetence that will bring me Big Mama's love. If I am helpless, she can help me. If I am strong, what good is she? This explanation is a cliché but nevertheless true. My mother made clichés come to life.

It was not in my best interest to be good, competent, strong, dynamic. Better to remain a helpless child, a weak incompetent male. Then she would love me. Strength and competence brought rejection, not applause. Since I love applause, you can understand my attraction to a life of helplessness.

3. The final thought is the possibility that my lower back hurts because I injured it doing something. But what did I do? Yoga demonstration for Rama? Speed running? Empty stomach exercise? Other?

I am moving towards one explanation: I am developing a new self-image, one of competence, excellence, strength, and skill; my lower back pain is protecting me from the psychological dangers of change by acting as a barrier.

Is that a smart thing to do, or does it represent my conservative animal self, hiding in its lair, protecting its young, fighting for survival against an overwhelming, unthinking monster? My lower back is the reactive repository of tradition, bulwark against change. Change can be constructive or destructive; in fact, creation and destruction work hand in hand. As my brain creates new self-images, my back resists them with old ones.

I will not be cured until I see my back pain as my friend.

I am chasing the will-of-the-wisp when I look to others for my salvation. As of today I am giving up my search for gods, and back pain with it; I'm turning back toward myself. It is the only safe haven. Whenever I leave the safety, security, and knowledge of believing in me, I move into a danger zone. Most of my mistakes have been made when I put my faith into the hands of others. Witness the stock market. When I put my trust in Joel's stocks, I lose money.

True, to balance it out, when I put trust my own stocks, I still lose money. Basically, the stock market has been a losing game for me. Perhaps this is precisely because I have put my faith in others. I am always buying companies I cannot possibly know much about. I read their balance sheets and study their histories, hopes, and plans for the future. Still, there is no way for me to know whether what they write is true. I only know the information they give me.

And I know about such information—and disinformation. I put it out myself when I am trying to sell tours, weekends, or folk dance classes. Some is true, some not; but at least when I lie, I know it. I have control over my lies. I have no control over the ones in annual reports. There is no way to tell if their balance sheets are correct, assets real, or liabilities greater than stated. I am taking a big chance buying them—and the head, back, and heartaches I get from losing money in stocks prove it. Life is a crap shoot. When I look within for guidance, I have a better chance at success.

Mitsubishi Madness

I raced up the highway, zoomed past malls on Route 4, zigzagged through the traffic lanes on route 17, crossed the great divide beyond Allendale, and entered Mitsubishi Country, where crones fly and mammoth lighting giants walk the skies in white shoes covered with furry fire.

I was on my way to get my Mitsubishi caliper pin. Bob Quirk and Todd, my mechanics, said the pin would halt the noise of fluid swishing in my brake system. I reached Ramsey Mitsubishi on Route 17 and walked in at exactly 5:05 p.m., wearing my Egypt hieroglyphic T-shirt and brown shorts. "Where's the parts department?" I asked the impeccably suited salesman sitting at the desk.

He pointed behind him. "Over there. But it's closed now."

"What?"

"They close at 4:30."

"You're kidding."

"They'll be open tomorrow at 8:00 a.m."

"What? I don't believe it. I've come all the way from Teaneck. I need that part by tomorrow. Isn't there a manager who can help me?"

"What part do you need?"

"A caliper pin for my 1987 Mitsubishi."

"You think they're going to bother opening up for a little thing like that? Forget it. Come back tomorrow."

"You're joking. What the fuck is the matter with this place? Shit! Shit! Shit! Why couldn't the parts guy have told me on the phone that they close at 4:30? What kind of shithole place closes at 4:30, anyway? Every professional place closes at five or six. I'm gonna report you. Oh, shit, shit, shit. This can't be happening to me. I drove like a maniac, rushed all this distance to find you assholes closed! I don't believe it."

"Believe it, sir. And kindly go fuck yourself. Come back tomorrow."

"I will, all right. . . with a bomb. I'm going to turn this Mitsubishi dump into Mit soup bishi."

"Please, sir, no violence. It distracts the customers."

I stormed out through the plate glass window.

Loving Business

How can I develop more confidence in what I do? Until now, every time I've gotten an idea, its opposite has immediately entered my head. Then the two ideas fight it out with each other until one wins. But it never wins completely, because its opposite lurks in the corner, ready to pounce and devour it. Positive ideas attack negative ideas; negative ones attack positive. The result is slow progress forward, like driving a car with the brakes on. Perhaps this is a wise method: It teaches caution. But at this point, I think it more a hindrance than anything else—an old negative that keeps invading my brain, trying to vitiate ideas I come up with. A bad habit.

Can I get rid of it? Easy to say, hard to do. But a worthy goal.

I am on a new upward path combining East and West, a blending of two great philosophic traditions. I have one good hour in the morning after coffee. That hour will be spent writing.

Then comes guitar, an hour of yoga or running, a light breakfast, and business. How can I pour purity, strength, oneness, and the love I have for the arts, writing, and guitar into business?

Love is the answer. All the philosophers, spiritual leaders, song writers, even psychologists, say love, love, love. No doubt, it rules the world. Big deal, though; the sun also rises every day. Does that mean I can unite myself with the energies of the sun? Not easily.

How do I introduce love into my business? I love teaching folk dancing, working with people, organizing them, moving them in the directions I want to go; I love writing, guitar, songs, arts, running, yoga, reading, studying, and languages.

Most of these are parts of my business. So what's stopping me from loving my business?

Is it voice from the past: my mother, father, relatives, friends, or acquaintances? None I can think of at the moment. The only person preventing me from loving my business is me.

Who is this "me" getting in my way? Why tolerate the antics of this shithead? I want to go to work each morning with enthusiasm. How great that would be!

Maybe I've always loved my business but refuse to recognize it. Rejection, and fear of financial ruin, have been the two great negatives in my business blocking me from loving it.

I don't experience them when I engage in any of my non-business pursuits—yet I constantly "make mistakes" as I practice them. Could I see business the same way?

On the path of love, one moves from darkness to light. Could my focus on rejection and financial ruin be "mistakes" too? Aren't they walls I create to block the light of love?

Art Is My Yoga

Was it the yoga breathing exercises that caused my panic? Or was it the idea that through yoga I will be "cured" of my writing habit, that I'll become a fully realized yogi like those living high in the Himalayas who live to be a hundred and sixty. These adepts are unknown to the public. They have given up the world.

Was this life of retreat and meditation my new dream goal? Does it have the ultimate answer to life's questions? If my panic is any signal, I doubt it. I am an artist first. I thrive on creativity, not retreats into unknown mountain regions. Mine is the way of karma yoga, the yoga of action. Who knows if I will live to a hundred sixty—and does it really make a difference, once you realize that time is an illusion and the material world is veiled by Maya?

Inspiration in Disguise

David, Jeannie, Zack, and Zane just arrived. Luckily my monster Buick had a battery so I could pick them up at the airport. They stuffed mucho pounds of luggage into the trunk. That's one.

Uncle Willie is in the hospital with a near-fatal virus, a rare kind of bacteria he picked up from a tick. He's in intensive care. Miki told me about it. I called Minna, where Mary is staying, then Jonny and Christie.

That's two.

I just got prices for my Greek Tour and Cruise in May from Cloud Tours. The land prices seem high. This is the second time Cally has come in with high prices. On Turkey, her first try, she came in higher than any Turkish tour company I deal with. Then, after I told her about it, she consulted her Turkish agents and lowered my price. I'll have to do research on prices. That means I won't be able to price my 1994-95 tours even though the brochure is coming out in a couple of weeks. That's not good. More than that, it raises the question in my mind: Can I trust Cally? Are her other prices too high? What about her judgement? She's recommending a standard hotel in Athens. She says it's charming. Is it? What does "charming" mean in her view? Will the price be way out of whack?

Trust is the bottom line when working with anybody. Trust, and belief in their good judgement. Without them there can be no business relationship, and probably no other kind. Cally seems like a nice woman, responsible and easy to work with. Maybe I'm wrong about her prices, but I doubt it.

That's three.

Otherwise I've got a great series of tours coming up in 1995. March will be Budapest and Prague—my favorite. Then May will be Greece—a new one. Finally, Cesary from Balkan Holidays told me that next August, 1995, there will be another Koprivshtitsa Folk Festival in Bulgaria! Wow! Koprivshtitsa takes place every five years. This one's coming a year earlier than I expected. In August I'll run a tour to Bulgaria and follow it with another one to Turkey. The Turkish itinerary will include Istanbul, Trabzon, Amasya, Cappadocia, and Ankara, with a visit to Gordium, all the places I wanted to visit this year but couldn't because our Turkish tour was cancelled due to low registration.

I'll promote Bulgaria as one tour, Turkey as another, and offer them back to back as a third option. Should be exciting: three great tours. I know them all.

I am writing about very concrete events. No philosophizing. I began the morning with an empty, down feeling, the one I usually call depression. It "forced" me to write. "Depression" may be a misnomer. The down feeling is an up feeling in disguise. Could depression really be elation in black clothing? It is the psychological equivalent of exhalation when the lungs are at their air-empty bottom and there is no place to go but up. Inhalation leads to full-fill-ment.

I should welcome these so-called "bad" feelings. In truth, I do.

Whenever Bernice tries to "cure" me of my downs, lows, complaints, and depressions, I always resist. What a puzzle. On the one hand, I whine about my miserable mental state, lousy business, lack of money, on and on; then, when she tries to soothe, understand, cure me, I resist. I find a reason to hold on to my so-called "illness." Now I see why. These lows are exactly what I always suspected they were: inspirations in disguise.

This depression-elation, exhalation-inhalation, process of the mind, which psychoanalysts often diminish by classifying it as manic depressive disease, is in actuality the oxygenating call of my creative life, a signal that creation is about to begin. Why should I give it up just because it feels unpleasant? Besides, I couldn't give it up even if I wanted to. If I did, I would get really depressed, and that would touch off another cycle of creativity.

If this roller coaster cycle is the source of creation in my artistic life, perhaps it is the same in my business life. Fear of financial failure, annoyance at lack of registration, anger and frustration when things go wrong in tours, weekends, or folk dance classes, all the pains that inhabit and inhibit my business life, push me to ask why I bother with all this shit. The entire mind-bending, frustrating mess is creativity once more rearing its ugly-beautiful head. I should welcome my states of misery. They are harbingers of higher things to come.

I am also taking a yoga class. Is it a metaphor of my future that my focus in this class is on pranayama, the art of yogic breathing?

Swami Rama calls pranayama the science of breath, but I like "art of breath" better.

Is breathing an art or a science? Probably both.

My next direction I will be the study of breathing. I'll focus on the inhalation–exhalation cycle of my artistic and business life.

The Heavenly Mountain

Since my mind won't give me a rest, my body has forced it on me. I felt a crunching pain in my lower back when I bent forward in the

Salutation to the Sun. Had I stopped, I would have saved two days of pain. If back pain is due to a muscle spasm, how about using the cobra asana? Would such a contrary stretch work? On the other hand, suppose back pain is, as John Sarno says, not a physical problem but a mental one? Suppose back pain is caused by a spasm from resistance, anger, or some other emotion?

I believe this is true. For the previous few days I had increased my yoga and running a great deal. I felt like I was at the top of my physical form; I was proud of myself! The superman complex was setting in again, even though I was on guard against it.

Suddenly, my back said no. Psychological, indeed. Sarno is absolutely right. I just find it hard to believe that it can happen to me. In fact, I can't believe it. Not a wise veteran runner-yogi like me. I have hurt my back so often, I know everything about it. I even give others advice on back pain. Therefore, such a slip cannot happen to me. I'm too smart for it.

Do I detect a hint of hubris? Indeed. But I have been on guard against even that, though I felt straight-jacketed by a compulsion to do more, push harder, even though I was tired. My master was too hard on me, though I am he. I am still angry at him. Why does he push me so hard? "Hey, give me a break. Let me take a day off without haunting my conscience. Surely I can have one day of rest."

"No, you cannot," says my master. "I am hard and unbending. I order you to follow your disciplines relentlessly and endlessly. There is no rest for you. Never, never! No break! You have too much to accomplish. You can rest after you die. Work, work, work, that is your ethic. You may get hurt in the process, but so what? I have no sympathy. Just because you make stupid mistakes and your mind fools you, then directs you down pathways of illusion, is no reason to ask me for sympathy. Forget 'days off.' Don't even think about them. My job is to whip you so you can climb the heavenly mountain. Laziness is not in my vocabulary. There are no 'short rests.' I will work you until you drop, and, after you sleep off your exhaustion and return to consciousness, I will grind you up with still more work. Stop being such a baby. What's a little back pain when the prize of the heavenly mountain is so close? You can hardly conceive of such rewards. Little weak boy, you should thank me for forcing you to push beyond yourself. You should even thank me for hurting your back. Back pain is simply another obstacle for you to overcome, another boulder blocking your upward path. It takes work to push boulders aside, but you will do it. You have no choice.

"A downward route exists, but I will not let you follow it. You were meant for higher things. I'm going to push you to the top whether you like it or not. Your back pain is a passing fly buzzing in your ear, a mosquito on your skin for a quick bite. These are transitory obstacles. I will not let you be deterred by them.

"We are moving beyond the borders of the known world."

This Weekend My Ego Did Me In

Fatigue came over me when I ran this morning. After ten minutes I simply stopped and walked. Then I thought, Maybe this fatigue is a prelude to higher consciousness. My fatigue stems from overuse. So does my pain-filled back. My intellect, prodded by my ego, pushed me to fill my exercise quota even though my body told me I needed a rest. Both fatigue and back pain come from an overabundance of ego. Had I listened to my intuition, I would have taken the day off. However, I am a fallible human being, prone to excesses.

"Hey, I'm only human." (The "I'm only human" crowd will excuse me for every miserable thing I do; it will also chase away my chances of improving.)

Instead of listening to that cry, reach for the higher calling of self-disgust.

"I'm disgusted with myself!"
"Dammit, I did it again!"
"What's the matter with me?"
"I'm such a moron."
"Won't I ever learn?"

These ego denigrations help you recognize the noxious, limited qualities of ego; they also nudge, cajole, and push you to rise above it.

Rather than something to cherish and worship, the ego is something to be overcome. Tough. . .but a worthwhile struggle. Ego is the gate-keeper of my crazed, wandering mind binging on self-improvement. And, this weekend, it did me in.

Goals

Suppose my desire for self-improvement is not a blessing, but a curse. Only the process of self-improvement has brought me happiness. Once I have arrived at my goal, I soon sink into despair.

I have based so much of my life on this search. If it's an illusion, then why bother with it? Yet what will I do with myself if I don't improve? What goals will I have? None. How can I live without goals? What will push me to get up in the morning?

Help—I Won't Impose

What is the secret of work, and of help? Do I help others when I work? If so, how?

These questions were raised by Vivekananda. I wonder: Am I of any use to anyone? I spend a great deal of time figuring out how to help myself. But I am not interested in others. Or am I?

Spiritual help is the highest form of service. It deals with the ever-lasting. Does what I do help others climb that ladder?

I like the vision of a ladder with spiritual help on top, intellectual help in the middle, and physical help at the bottom. On the surface, this vision means I don't really have to help anybody. I can just keep doing my own thing trying to improve myself, and stop worrying about others. I have control over myself, but as for others, who says they want to be helped in the first place? Most people just want to be left alone. They don't care about this spiritual stuff: "Buy me a hamburger, and don't forget the onions."

And who can blame them?

I don't like people who are constantly trying to teach, improve, or tell me what's right. I let them go their own way.

That's my way of helping them. By leaving them alone, I believe I am doing them a great service— providing the opportunity to discover how to do things on their own. By not badgering them, letting them fail or succeed by themselves, I am showing they have the power.

Life is a grand experiment and adventure. I'm not going to take the thrills away from you by imposing my own attitudes and improvements.

You don't need my help at all. The ups and downs will be all yours; you will ride your own roller coaster, learning whatever you have to from it.

I'll be around if you need me.

But you'll have to ask. I won't impose. Anything but that. I've had too much of that in my life already.

More Goals

I'd like to come back from Cape Cod with some new goals for the 1994–95 season. But I can't find any. I latched onto learning how to read and write Sanskrit. This would be a good adjunct to studying Yoga and would certainly help me understand basic Indian philosophical works such as the Vedas, Upanishads, Vedanta, etc. I may do this. But once again I feel like I've been through something similar before. I don't get a gut-wrenching, stomach-churning reaction. Not much pain either. I think back to when I started my guitar career or running tours. Now there were gut-wrenching, stomach-churning, tension, nervousness, sleepless nights, fears, anxiety, and mucho worry. That was *living!* Now I've conquered many of my fears. I'm cured. . . but bored. I'd love to move on to some high- minded, nearly impossible goal. But what? I've started writing, running, yoga; yesterday, as I played, I realized I had passed beyond my guitar breakthrough. I was in the integrating phase. From now on I'll be playing well.

What do I aim for now? I need to keep myself interested and awake in life. If I can't *find* any new goals, I'd better make them up.

Will those motivate me? Will I do anything without divine guidance? Usually a new challenge must be revealed to me. It swoops down from the heavens in a divinely inspired, flashing moment. Suddenly, I know! That's what happened with guitar. I didn't ask, expect, or even hope for it. One day it just happened: a visit from His Majesty.

The same thing happened when my Turkish tour was cancelled. Through divine help I decided to devote my summer to writing, training for a marathon, and guitar practicing. I did; it worked.

But nothing new in writing. Every day more of the same, page after page of unedited *New Leaf.*

No qualitative changes here. But I keep ploughing ahead. I may have to write for twenty- five more years before a message comes down from His Majesty raising me to a higher level.

New directions on a horizontal plane are out for now. I'm moving vertically, towards intensity, focus, and concentration.

Can depth plunging replace the excitement of horizontal travel? Isn't there some new world for me to conquer on the lateral plane? How about stomach churning and gut-wrenching insecurity? It used to drive me on. If I don't believe in it anymore, what will replace it? I don't like being afraid. But without anxieties, what will motivate me?

Clouds in Transit

I'm concentrated on Indian philosophy, especially Buddha's Four Noble Truths, the Eightfold Path, and how to end human suffering.

Is it possible? I could start with my own. Never mind everyone else's. They are free to suffer on their own time.

Buddha says free yourself from desire for the fruits of your action. Bananas, apples, oranges, pears, plums—not one fruit should I want. Want a fruit, get a pain.

I'll start by trying to renounce some favorite fruits: guitar performing, the desire to publish or run a marathon. I'll move on to yearning after more customers and more money in the stock market. Will this calm the fluctuations of my mind?

Do I really want a calm mind? What about all the fun I have when it goes up or down, the hidden joys of depression, thrill of anger, excitement of rage, sweet longings for success, happy dreams of adulation and fame from fans who love my work?

Well, why not accept them? Earthly ups and downs are fun; even misery has a plus side. I am ready to move vertically, descending to depths and rising to heights.

Life's cycles are clouds in transit. The calm mind smooths ripples on the lake, making visible the infinite bed.

The Swoon

Where is the beauty in yoga postures? In the swoon.
The experience of beauty tingles throughout your body.

The Art of Play

I get up about five or six, have coffee, and do all the important things. By eleven I'm finished. That's when my descent begins. Soon I am in the blackest hole. I don't know why. Nothing has really changed except my attitude towards life.

This miserable period lasts until about three, when I slowly begin to pick up again. Soon a new shot of energy carries me until about seven o'clock. Then I am truly satisfied and finished for the day.

But I don't understand the afternoon downs—more important, don't know how to stop them.

Yesterday I had a private yoga class with Rama. I asked questions about breathing, pranayama, and these downs. He suggested I take a walk, read, sleep, let my mind relax and tune in to the creative process. Then I realized what I should do: nothing. When I was a kid, after practicing violin or doing homework, I'd go out and play. Can playing still work?

By eleven I'm physically and mentally drained; I need a rest. But I won't give myself a rest. Instead, I mope around, mentally beating myself because I can't accomplish more, improve something, practice, sell more tours, weekends, or folk dance classes. Instead of doing that, I'll play at doing nothing. It is a most difficult art form for adults.

Running Yoga Postures

Excellent long run at the farm yesterday. I did part of it as a "yoga posture." I "held the posture" as I ran, breathing in for three counts, out for three counts, and tying each count to a step. A three-count inhalation to three steps, a three-count exhalation to three steps. When I got faster I did a two-count inhalation to two steps and two-count exhalation to two steps. For warm-ups, I did a four-count inhalation for four steps and a four-count exhalation for four steps.

By focusing on these counts, I hypnotized myself as I ran. If I took my mind off the counts, I would break my rhythm and stop running.

I was pushing myself! Oh, yes! At a semitorture level. Watch out for injury. I could get a heart attack and die. I could tear an Achilles tendon or do irreparable damage to some part of my body and end my folk dancing career forever. I thought about medical insurance, how I could pay all my hospitable bills after the life-threatening injury that occurred because I'd run too much or too fast. I kept creating one negative thought after another, and as I did I could feel my chest tightening up, my breath coming shorter, myriad new aches and pains in my body. As I kept shooting negative arrows into myself, I felt my energies collapsing right and left.

Then I thought, Stop creating negatives. Today there is no reason to get injured or be tired. I am well rested. I'm putting aside my negative thoughts and substituting a running yoga posture.

At the beginning of the big hill I ran slightly faster, counting my breaths, first in fours, then, as I went faster, in threes. Soon, I ran my maximum speed in twos. I'd done it! Moving beautifully, I got as far as the Downsville dam, turned around, and headed back. Negative thoughts returned—I'll die because I ran so fast; my body aches because I'm getting old; I'm finished as a runner, folk dancer, and physical specimen—and I moved through aching quadriceps and chest-heaving discomfort. Again I focused: Go beyond negative thoughts. Think elation, higher forces; concentrate on the higher energies of running yoga postures.

I'd done it! My mind cleared; my pains went away. I concentrated on the count, my breathing, my posture, on the idea that yogis can turn pain into pleasure and ecstasy. Concentrating, concentrating, I made it straight up the big hill without stopping. I went further on the flat ground, still concentrating on the count, moving slowly down from twos to threes to fours.

Then I broke the count, got tired immediately, stopped running, and started walking. I realized my sudden fatigue had occurred because I'd broken the rhythm of my count. I resumed the rhythm, and started running again. Fours, threes, then twos, I headed onward. I stopped once more, then made it home.

This long run opened new doors. It showed me the frightening potential of my power, the awesome effect of positive thoughts and how to use the yoga posture approach to life's problems. Not bad for one day.

The Good Foot Hope

Do I have a wart on my foot? Or is a splinter?

Yesterday I went to my podiatrist, Dr. McNierney. He looked at it, called it an impossible name, and said it was caused by an imbalance in the sesamoid bone. Then he used knives, scissors, and other implements, and, as I thought about the relationship between screaming and yoga meditation, dug it out of my foot.

He gave me a new orthotic, a depressing lecture on how my feet would get worse in time, and that although wearing orthotics would not cure me, at least they would slow the inevitable decay.

Could I run on the streets or walk around the house without the orthotic? I asked. Impossible, he said. McNierney is not a mystic. I hope for miracles, but he says my foot will only get worse. He could be right.

But he could be wrong. He knows about his patients; he doesn't know about miracles—or at least believe in them. But I do, and I'll work towards it, too. McNierney may be right about the ultimate decay of my foot, but why should I believe him? Maybe he's wrong. Maybe there's some higher knowledge that he doesn't know about. My wishes and hopes are pitted against his years of practical experience. Maybe both of us are right.

Vivian, with her knowledge of Chinese medicine, said, "Try running without the orthotic, try walking without it, and see how it feels—listen to your body." I liked her Chi Kung philosophy. It gave me hope.

I am torn between hope and Dr. McNierney's fixed views. Can hope cure a foot? Maybe it's more important than a good foot.

Bumpy Morning

The lamp on my desk is flickering. What the fuck is wrong with it? I'm taking it to Dason's Lamp Store today. Let them check it out. So annoying to write and have that fucking thing flickering in the midst of my inspirations. God damn, now it's *out!*

What a pain in the ass; at least it gives me something to write about. Little things are going wrong this morning. Minor annoyances. Like my Mitsubishi brakes.

I've spent hundreds of dollars trying to find out what's wrong with them and fix them. Now they're malfunctioning again. This means yet another trip to Quirks to check them out. Will he ever find out what's wrong? Now the light has stopped flickering. Is this a respite?

MONEY AND ITS BRETHREN

Performance and Sales are Synonymous

Business is very dead now. No money is coming in, and money is going out at the usual mini-rapid rate.

Yesterday Joel, my stock broker, said I was taking too much time off, that I needed some productive, money-making work to do along with my non-monetary activities. I agreed.

But agreement is a far cry from actually doing something. I like what I am doing, even though none of it pays any money.

I decided a few months ago that money comes from God. Stop worrying about money, I said. Just do your work, and money will come—and go. If you are still worried, think about death. Death solves all financial problems.

But worrying about money is my prime disease. It freezes me. I end up walking around the block in a frenzy.

My mind invents new and future fears of financial ruin and devastation. I was put on earth to create, not have such concerns; they're an unnatural state.

In any case, until I can think of a new business or business direction, I'm going to put aside my worries, travel my road, and take whatever adventures come along.

One of them might even be lucrative.

Order

I am disgusted with the organizational sloppiness of my life. It does not fit my compulsive character. Hundreds of journal pages, therapy hours, and walks around the block, deep in thought, have been spent on "why?" I'm finished with it now. Done and disgusted. I don't want to look at that old sloppy disheveled rebellious self. I am leaving psychotherapy and babble land for good. Goodbye, kaput, and done. I want organization; I want character; I want to pay off all my debts. My vacation is over. On one level, it has lasted fifteen years. On another, it started this June when I put together my Miracle Schedule. I developed the habit of daily writing, guitar playing, running, doing yoga, and language study. They remind me of the spiritual foundation of my life and put me in touch with higher forces.

But they don't bring in hard cash. I don't want to be bullied, pushed, shoved, and tossed about by financial fears. But I do need money. I must put my finances in order. Financial order symbolizes mental order; since I love order in the spiritual world, I want it in my material world as well. That means making bucks and paying off my debts. How do I do that? Money As an End-In-Itself. I haven't thought about making money since last May. I had put it aside for the summer. Now what? I'm going back to the city. I want to take some new attitude with me. Will it have something to do with money?

Money has always been a means to an end for me, the end being freedom and happiness. That's why I have mixed feelings about it. I have focused, not on the act, but the fruit of the action.

If I'm going to change my thinking about money, I'll have to view it as an end in itself. Wouldn't that end my conflict about it?

One of the ways to do so might be in terms of mathematics and pure numbers. In some mystic philosophies, numbers are goods in themselves.

They represent the cosmic forces.

The integer "1" is God Himself. By balancing the numbers I could be balancing ego and other, art and business, self and universe. What about passion? Can it fit into numbers?

PERFORMANCE

Nervousness Before the Dawn

When I lead folk dancing I get nervous before each class, but not as nervous as before a guitar concert. I spend several hours in preparation. Mentally, I call up my energies, focus my mind on the class, put myself in the mood by improvising a csárdás. Then, an hour before the class, I go over specific dances and loosely prepare a program.

Folk dance classes and guitar concerts are performances. Both make me nervous. How about tours? Sometimes they make me nervous for a year as I prepare for them. It seems I get nervous before any challenge I face. Nervousness is part of my energy pattern.

The question is: how to use it? Improving my skills does not make me any less nervous. It only means I have a higher standard to maintain. I am secretly proud of this, secretly a hero. Look, folks, how I suffer in order to grow! I push, squeeze, and beat myself to reach a higher level. But I don't want to boast too loudly about my suffering; others might be jealous or think I'm sick. It's macho and masculine to struggle, fight, and suffer, especially for such a worthy cause. After all, what else do I have to live for besides reaching for the stars? When I grab one, I feel great! But soon other stars appear. Then I want to expand, reach out to new galaxies.

Thus this business of trying to "cure" my nervousness is a total waste of time. Let's face it: I like to suffer. It makes me feel great! Often at the end of my struggle, the sun of satisfaction shines on me and I am blessed.

Basic Assumptions

It's amazing how fast one can degenerate. Last Thursday when I left for the Paramount Hotel, I was flying high. All my disciplines were in place. But under the pressure of a long work weekend I "forgot" them. Saturday, Sunday, and Monday I did nothing. Tuesday morning, I woke up feeling down. Where did all the fulfillment of performing these satisfying tasks go?

Nevertheless, I accomplished a lot on the weekend. I decided to go back to performing! How and why this occurred this weekend, I do not know. Perhaps I was simply ready. In any case, I gave my first performance in a year. I was just as nervous as when I performed last year, the year before, and twenty years ago. Nothing has changed on that score. So be it. I am back in the fight.

Practicing and knowing what I am doing has hardly helped at all. Performance anxiety is evidently not a technical problem but an emotional one. It has to do with the way I look at the world, the way I look at the audience. I start out with the basic assumption the audience wants to destroy me. This is my big negative. Years of practicing have not changed it. Could I possibly change this through cognitive therapy? Bernice says yes. Her comments were excellent, the best in years. Through just a few good sentences she has redeemed herself. Maybe she does better therapy on her patients than on me. Whatever, her positive comments were a ray of hope in my black view of performance misery.

Suppose I could change my fundamental view of the audience—assume the audience will love me and love whatever I perform? This would be a major miracle. I can hardly imagine it. My nervousness occurs, not just when I perform on guitar, but extends to almost everything I do in front of others, whether it is teaching folk dancing, running a weekend or tour, or even entering a room full of people. It so happens I have a talent with people, and once I get warmed up I'm okay with them. Once I'm past the door of fear, I'm funny and lively and enjoy playing the social game. But getting past that door is tough. It generally takes about twenty minutes to warm up.

Could I change my basic assumptions about the audience? Do I want to?

Maybe I like being nervous. It makes me feel victimized and heroic at the same time; I become special, unique, and outstanding in my misery.

Am I ready to change my attitude?

Yes! There must be a better way, even though I don't know what it is.

Performing Is My Bridge

If depression is the prelude to creation, I've got a creative day coming. I'm doing a reading at the Teaneck Library. I've been going over the *New Leaf* prose I've written since January. What should I choose from this five-hundred-page mass?

My first decision is: I am not going to read from New Leaf. It puts too much pressure on me to find a reading. I've already got prose poems in my other three books. This is my first reading, my debut. Why not go with what I know? Why not the best? I could use tried and true readings like "Chickens" and "A True Fan" in *Handfuls of Air* with new ones from *Crusader Tours*.

I'll probably go that route. I've got to practice my new readings, read them into a tape recorder, listen and analyze, then time it. It's a performance, folks. I'd like it to be good. This means performing the best I can while remembering to desire and expect nothing from the audience—a difficult but worthy goal.

What purpose does an audience serve?

If it is my job to serve them yet desire and expect nothing from them, why have them there in the first place? Perhaps their purpose is to push, stimulate, and inspire me to rise higher. Like the veil of Maya, they force me to face the illusion of their existence while simultaneously struggling to give my best.

In a larger, mystical sense, I am my audience. Ultimately, I will see them as an extension of myself. I will look beyond their faces and physical bodies, their fleshy embodiments, and feel the unity of their spiritual existence. But before I can see this I must conquer my fears.

The Upside to Unworthiness

Why am I a performer? To prove that I am worthy? If that is the case, performing doesn't work. No matter how many times I "prove" myself before an audience, my temporary high soon sinks back to the same question. I was born singing the "Am I Worthy?" song. It is one of my birthmarks. Years of psychoanalysis, self-study, guitar practice, concerts, running tours, weekends, teaching folk dance classes, reading history and philosophy, have not answered this basic unworthy question.

Maybe I will never change.

Maybe it's a positive question. There is an upside to unworthiness. It forces me to keep perfecting myself. If I was worthy, why bother?

My Love Affair with Nervousness Is Over

Freedom without discipline leads to anarchy.

I just got back from the Smorgasbord Weekend at Solways. What a triumph on all levels! I gave my first yoga class. A success! I prepared my concert program for three days. A success! Biggest success of all: I was not nervous! I have given up my love affair with nervousness.

This is a major triumph. Not that I wasn't concerned. I spent three days thinking about my concert, going over the pieces, planning it from beginning to end. When I gave the concert, I was ready. I discarded my planned program, tuned in to the mood of the audience, and moved with the flow.

I don't know why I gave up my love affair with nervousness. Maybe I was just "ready."

I used to think nervousness was one of my fundamental motivating forces, pushing me to work even when I didn't want to. But it was simply an obstacle posing as a useful protective cover that I had to overcome. Looking back, I can't see any benefits in performance anxiety. All it did was silence my enthusiasm. Understanding my problem is easy; solving it may take a lifetime.

I added readings to my concert, too. A reading voice goes well with the voice of a classical guitar—it expresses a pensive evening program symbolizing a new direction.

Guitar As Meditation

A new leap on the guitar and writer's path this morning. It all started when I read the introduction to Mantra and Meditation, by Pandit Usharbudh Arya. It was written by Sri Swami Rama, one of my favorites. He said that, in Western tradition, the Bible clearly states: "Be still and know that I am God."

Then he said, "In meditation, one has to learn to be still first. This begins with a physical stillness."

That's when the idea struck me. Yoga teaches stillness through asanas, and stillness through breathing exercises—pranayama. This leads to meditation. Then I thought: could guitar practicing be meditation, a form of inner stillness discipline? Could I find inner peace and silence as I pluck each note, slowly, carefully, gracefully, listening to the tone I produce, paying complete attention, as mentally I watch the string slide from my fingertip across my fingernails, and see the sound itself spring from the sound hole, travel the air waves, enter my ear, and calm my mind?

Audience and performance technique would be secondary; the primary purpose of my guitar would be an aid to meditation.

Intriguing idea. My deeply ingrained habit of early morning practice opens me, tunes me to the world as it wakes my sleepy body and brain. Fist thing in the morning, I find it almost impossible to practice traditional yoga exercises like Salute to the Sun, breathing, or even sitting meditation. I've tried them all; all have fallen by the wayside. But morning guitar playing is easy and has lasted years. It is a habit formed during my teens that has never left me. It is my natural medium. Using guitar as meditation is an original thought. Nowhere in any of the literature on yoga does this suggestion occur.

Can such an original idea work for me? Can my thoughts be trusted? I'll ask Rama what he thinks. But am I really asking him for permission to believe what I believe? Suppose he says, "No, it is absolutely wrong. One cannot use guitar for meditation. Only tradition techniques can be used. Give up your stupid notion; go back to the basics described in the Yoga Sutras of Pantanjali." He wouldn't say that, but suppose he did? I would consider it, even try it, then "sink" back to my original thoughts. Obviously, I will end up doing what I want anyway, even though my questions and self-doubts make me take a little longer. Generally my instincts are right for me.

I'll invent a new meditation form. Perhaps once upon a time, high in the Himalayas, a yogi wearing a loin cloth sat on his pillow in full lotus position, meditated, did pranayama, and played the guitar—but his unique meditation practice never made the yoga books. I may be following his ancient tradition. In any case, I'll just have to creep along, following the ant's trail as I cautiously inch my way towards enlightenment.

But it is more than that. Vis-á-vis yoga, I am in the position I was when I asked the folk dance question: Which steps are right? How much can I improvise and choreograph and still be faithful to the folk dance traditions? I didn't want to just do my "own thing" in a vacuum and call it a folk dance. I wanted to base my choreographies and improvisations on knowledge of folk traditions. The questions, "How do people in these foreign countries dance?" and "How free can I be to improvise?" led to the creation of my Folk Tours business. Now I feel the strength of knowledge in my folk dance inventions, but it took ten years of tours to Bulgaria, Hungary, Czechoslovakia, Israel, Egypt, Soviet Union, Turkey, and Ireland to get it.

Now I'm asking the same questions about yoga. How much can I improvise and adopt for myself? Will it still be "yoga" when I am through? What are the limits to my freedom? Where does it turn into anarchy? I can't answer these questions in a vacuum. I have to study, learn, explore, and ask mucho questions. Rama is one of the places to start.

Great Guitar Playing!

Great guitar playing! I've made the ultimate breakthrough! I've been using the tape recorder to record my practicing, then listening to it. What a teacher! In some pieces, I'm not as bad as I thought; in others, worse.

It started a few weeks ago when I listened to my playing of Villa-Lobos's "Prelude Number 4." It gave me confidence.

This week I practiced "Alard." I played it ten times a day. Suddenly, I was playing it well! Fast! With passion! How beautiful it sounded on the tape! Then I thought, if I can play the "Alard," how about "Alhambra?" Sure enough, I listened to my playing and discovered my problem. For years I have been emphasizing the treble; Segovia emphasized the base. After years of rebelling against Segovia, I finally agreed he was right. As soon as I emphasized the base, focused on the base line, my playing leaped forward, improving dramatically.

Today I added Leyenda and the flamencan dances, emphasizing the base line on all my arpeggios. It worked! I couldn't believe it when I played it back on the tape recorder. Every tremolo improved; so did the scale passages. I improved.

This is all too exciting to believe. After years of struggling, going round in the same circles, I have finally broken through. I will be a great guitarist. I will have the enthusiasm and passion for playing and performing. I may even play at parties for nothing or just pick up someone's guitar in their home and play it for others.

The Doctrine of Divine Sloppiness, or Transcending the Notes

I've had a miraculous performance breakthrough in the past few days—so much so, I gave up writing for awhile. What happened is basically indescribable. I transcended the notes. I played with gusto, abandon, and incredible speed. Best of all, I discovered and formulated the Doctrine of Divine Sloppiness. When I play guitar with this in mind, I can't miss, because I'm transcending the notes. Whether I phlumf a note, skip a few, or miss half the trebles in my tremolo, it all doesn't matter, since my purpose is to transcend the score. That's the Doctrine: Concentrate on the divine. Missing no-tes is besides the point.

What about forgetting notes? Impossible. With the Doctrine of Divine Sloppiness, if I forget a passage I just stick in another one. As long as I stay on the transcendent plain, changed, forgotten, or mistaken notes hardly mean a thing.

What a marvelous release! A miracle! It has taken about eighteen years to reach this state. The chai years of life. But it could have taken thirty years or even a lifetime. I can look for explanations forever of why this miracle has occurred now, but I'll only find partial reasons. The quantum leap, the jump from quantity to quality, to a new level of guitar playing on a different plane: Suddenly, I have joined the masters. I can stand with Julian Bream, Andres Segovia, and other great guitarists I worshiped in my past. I can stand with them different but equal. Is it hubris to say so? When I played passages with breathtaking speed and fiery passion, I didn't think so. I stood with the gods in that heavenly circle.

Yes, Ma, that's me standing there. I finally made it! It's so strange that this miracle occurs at the end of my Book of Performance. I take credit for the years of practicing, of suffering on stage—trying, trying, trying, and never giving up. But the breakthrough was nevertheless a gift of grace bestowed on me by God Himself. How else could it have happened? I have the power to work hard and follow my disciplines, but not to create miracles.

Guitar Breakthrough

This morning I played the guitar—gloriously, wondrously beyond the descriptions of mortal speech. Tears danced in my eyes as perfected "Alhambras," dizzying "Bulerias" and "Leyendas," sprang from the instrument. I was in shock. I may remain in shock for weeks. . . or it may end tomorrow. It does not matter. The beauty of cascading arpeggios sounding clear and true, and the dazzling possibilities of such incredible dexter facility are miraculous and unbelievable to me. I don't recognize myself. Who is playing these lighting scales, these dazzling arpeggios? Could it be me? There's no one else in the room.

I cannot explain this breakthrough. But I am going to ride it, get used to the new me, solidify my gains, and turn today's miracle into an everyday occurrence, to insure that my playing breakthrough does not leave me. I have jumped up to a new level. I don't want to slip back down again.

My priorities have changed. My main effort will now go into guitar. I've worked over twenty- five years to play it this way. Now that I see the sun above me, I'm sticking around for a tan.

This morning I moved beyond Bream and Segovia, entered a plane where dwells the music of the spheres.

Confirmation

Bernice and Sue welcomed me to Cape Cod. We all went out to dinner with the Sakheims and Wanders. I sat next to Marilyn. We had a conversation that made my day.

I told her about my guitar breakthrough. "It's a miracle," I said. "I don't understand why it happened. I'm afraid it might go away. Part of me believes I'm moving to another level, and part of me says how stupid I am to have taken twenty-five years to achieve this break-through. How did it happen? Why did it happen? Can I believe my experience? It this dream too good to be true?"

I wanted someone to confirm my experience. Marilyn did just that. She said a similar "miracle" was happening to her in tennis. After forty-five years, her serve had "suddenly" improved. I didn't understand or care about the technicalities, but that even after forty-five years a break-through can still occur.

Marilyn's experience verified my own. My guitar progress is real and irreversible. A miracle took place. God stepped in—and so did I. I practiced day after day, week after week, month after month, year after year. I never stopped working. Even though I wanted to give up countless times, went through years of frustration, I kept at it. Practice, practice, practice, for fifteen years, twenty. Often I felt I was standing still. No matter what I tried, I couldn't play a tremolo or my favorite pieces like "Alhambra," "Leyenda," the flamencan dances, Villa-Lobos "Prelude No. 4," and "Alard." I got nowhere. I practiced these pieces slowly, then more slowly; I practiced them fast, then faster. I tried re-laxation, tension, accents, no accents, rest stroke, free stroke, breathing into the notes, and breath retention. I tried anything and everything for years and years. Nothing worked. How frustrating! During that period my desire to perform and my performances slid to just about zero. But I kept practicing. It was a habit I couldn't break—and I loved the physical feel of the guitar in my hands. Just because I couldn't per-form publicly or play my Achilles-heel "Alhambra" didn't mean I couldn't sit in a solitary corner in my house and "play for myself."

This summer I started yoga lessons with Rama. I asked him what I should practice. He said, "Work on postures you're not good at, espe-cially the forward bend."

This seemed like good advice. After focusing on the forward bend for a few days I was bending further forward than ever before. Im-provement through focus and concentration! Then I thought, Why not apply this kind of intense focus to my guitar? With the words of Rama echoing in my mind, I began a focus campaign aimed at playing the "Alard." In one day I played it about fifteen times. To my surprise, the next day, it had improved immeasurably. On the following day, I was playing up to speed! I recorded it on the tape recorder. I sounded like Segovia. Next day, even better!

This was absolutely amazing. I thought, If such focus and concentration work for "Alard," maybe they will work for "Alhambra." I tried the same technique. Sure enough, after a couple of days, the walls of the "Alhambra" crumbled and I entered the citadel. Wow! Incredible! I began applying the focus technique to my other pieces, even scale passages in "Bulerias" and "Zapateado." My blazing fingers flew. What was happening? Why now? I couldn't believe it.

When you are ready to learn, your teacher will appear. I was ready to learn. Rama was my teacher. He appeared.

He only spoke one sentence: "Work on postures you're not good at." That was enough. I was ready to hear it. I'm still hearing it. I'm just beginning to believe the results, too.

My guitar breakthrough proves that, by practicing over and over again, sticking with it, a qualitative chance will one day occur and lift you to a higher plane. Plant seeds in darkness; eventually a garden will bloom.

BUSINESS

Hopeful Birth of Creative Marketing

There is nothing like a cup of morning coffee to give you an optimistic morning rush. I want to love marketing. But the more I want to love it, the more I hate it. This is an ongoing conflict. As the summer moves along and I reflect on the exciting tours I've run in the past, I ask myself: If they were so wonderful, why not do more of them? Naturally, I've forgotten all the heartache involved. But nevertheless, the challenge, desire, hope, and more have gone out of tours.

What problem can challenge and transform me the way organizing my tours once did?

Marketing. I hope it becomes a calling.

I can only hope the call comes loud and clear, or, if not, then in small-stepped whimpers.

Stretching

My folk dancers need yoga. Almost none of them stretch after dance class. Even Ginny, who is a folk dance teacher and took Vivian's Chi Kong class, has dropped the exercises. Sid Wenokor's body is falling apart because he doesn't stretch or do yoga-type exercises. He says he is not disciplined enough; he hates the idea of exercise. Yet he loves tennis. "Tennis isn't exercise," he says, "it's something I love. Exercise is self-torture for self-improvement." No wonder he hates it.

Just got back from my last night of teaching at Goldensbridge. How I love that group! What a great job! Not only is it good money, but the mix of people cannot be found in any other group I teach. Kids, old people, beginners, advanced, they all show up and dance together. It is dripping hot in the social-hall barn with fans blowing and making humming whirring noise so you can hardly hear the music without turning up the volume. People everywhere are dripping, sweat pouring out of every pore. Because, or in spite, of it, the dancing rises to lofty heights. The stifling heat only makes it better. The old wooden barn floor is kissing soft, caressing the feet and putting smiles on dancer's faces. In short, a great night.

Too bad my job ended. Too bad my Turkish tour was also cancelled for lack of people. I'm sorry about the money I'm not going to make. It scares me because I'm sinking further into debt. And with my stocks descending to new lows each day, it makes for a discouraging August. I'll soon have to pay for mailing and publicity expenses, plus our upcoming vacation in Cape Cod. The kids are coming in from Santa Fe. More expenses.

Courage and hope are truly the most important attitudes. Remember: Money is never as important as spirit.

I left Goldensbridge high from a night of beautiful dancing, but disoriented about the future.

I've got to get back to writing. This because it is good for my mind, soul, spirit, and, hopefully, someday for business. Arlene and I are preparing the 1994–95 brochure. I just organized our first Folk Dance and Yoga Weekend with Rama and Rajam Ramanathan teaching yoga. I wrote the copy for the flier. I liked it. No more bending and twisting my sentences to please an imaginary audience who might register for a weekend, folk dance class, or tour. I don't even know these imaginary people. Why should I write for them? I've always hated writing advertising copy, because my mind is on what I think others want me to say rather than what I want to say. It's taken years to write copy in my own off-the-wall way. If people like it, fine; if not, that's okay, too. The pleasure of writing in my own style more than offsets their dislike. Besides, if they don't like what I write, who wants them, anyway? My customers must not only like me and what I offer but have part of their brain hanging out in left field so we have something in common like pieces of gray matter drifting off into space. Those unhinged elements of their personalities are the parts that will plug into the folk dance Mutual Unhingement Society. Members of this society will become the core customers of my business.

I am asking something from my customers. What can you offer me? How much of your energy, time, and enthusiasm are you willing to give to me?

I'm not interested in miserable, part- time, paltry one-shot commitments. I want more from you—not only your money and your time, but your soul as well. Yes, I want to grab you in the kishka, the gut, and drag your entrails across the dance floor, up to flying Catskill Mountain weekends, across the ocean on tours to fabled foreign lands. I want souls who yearn for this release. I expect you to lay out good cold cash for the privilege of making yourself healthy by walking the path of transcendence.

What chutzpa I have to demand such commitments from paying customers!

What a welcome change from wanting to bend over backwards to please them. Now I want them to please me and pay for the privilege. I love it! I should have done this ages ago, but of course I didn't have the confidence. But there has been a landslide. I'm sick and tired of trying to please the vast lackluster body of unenthusiastic potential customers who never show up for anything anyway.

My writing points my way to spontaneity, jumping ideas, and the intimate abuse of my already pulverized brain.

Beginner Folk Dance Franchise

I need a grandiose, glorious, world-shattering business dream.

Is it creating beginner folk dance classes?

I will dream the dream of growing beginner classes throughout the metropolitan area; I will have teachers working for me. This will create a new folk dance market as well as new customers to go on weekends and tours.

My Monday night beginner course will be the prototype of other beginner courses. I will expand like a folk dance franchise.

The folk dance market has to be built from the bottom up.

Exhalation and Inhalation

It's a sad day. . . and I love it. I am sad because I've been so successful. The Smorgasbord Weekend was a smash hit: I even made more money on the weekend than I expected.

Sadness comes from believing in success.

What is that but fulfillment of purpose, of a promise, a complete inhalation?

Where do you go once you've inhaled? Exhale, of course. The

lungs deflate on their return passage towards emptiness. I deflate, moving from fulfillment and success towards emptiness. Thank God for that; I like the fullness of air in the lungs, but only for awhile. I need sinking, too. Only the emptiness will push me to write and work towards fulfillment again. By nature I am more of an artist than a meditator.

Divine Indifference Among the Weeds of Teaneck Maya

Last night we got home from the Cape. Mucho mail and phone calls as usual. I got a call from Francine at the Riverdale Y telling me my classes can't start September 21 because the Y is closed for the Jewish holidays. Instead I must start October 5. This call destroyed the yogic calm and divine Buddhalike indifference I had been cultivating at Cape Cod. What the fuck is wrong with her? We spoke about this date last June, and she okayed it. I've sent out a mailing to fifteen hundred people announcing September 21 as our opening night in Riverdale. It's even listed as opening September 21 in the Y's bulletin.

The idiot! I'll call her today. Maybe it's a mistake.

Perhaps it is also a test. Maintaining a yogic calm is easy at Cape Cod. But can I maintain my divine indifference as I struggle for business survival in the weeds of Teaneck Maya?

Helping Others Through Divine Selfishness

When people say they want to help others, usually they want to help themselves by helping others. That sounds like a fair deal.

Can ecstasy help others? Can art open doors? I believe in divine selfishness.

Whatever light I create on my path to enlightenment may accidently shine on others. That is the only form of helping I know.

Focusing on others is often just an excuse, a foil, to get my mind off myself. I can't stand thinking about myself. Yet that's mostly all I do. I'd like to move beyond this state.

I Cure Myself by Helping Others

My folk dance classes started yesterday. I was nervous. When I picked up the heavy boxes of brochures at Jim Fessel's, I thought I'd hurt my back.

Sure enough, an hour later my back started to hurt. By the time I got to St. Paul's Church, I could hardly move. As I limped towards the bathroom, I thought of the words conversion hysteria. Suddenly, I knew what was wrong: I was nervous! Damn it!

I'd just spent a week at Cape Cod dwelling on the Absolute union with the Divine, meditating on the higher spiritual forms through yoga, vedanta, advaita philosophy, nondualism. . .and as soon as I return to work, I'm nervous. Failed again.

No matter how much philosophy, religion, or spirituality I study, nervousness does not go away. Instead of feeling better, anxiety metamorphoses into a back, knee, or ankle ache; I've only succeeded in fooling myself.

But the music cured me. I heard those gorgeous Israeli horas, Romanian bruils, and American ragtime dances. As I danced, I broke down crying from the pain and beauty of music. I thought, How lucky I am!

Music is my god, my entrance to the divine.

Why look elsewhere?

Forget about Ramakrishna or anyone else. As the tears fell last night, the pain in my lower back melted away; I thanked God and Beethoven and all the musicians and composers of the world for creating their cures.

I also thought, How lucky I am to have these folk dance classes and people that dance with me. I should thank them all. They are part of what cures me.

My students force me out of my retreat into myself, out of the pitfalls on the paths of mysticism and ecstasy. They push me beyond my ego. I cure myself by helping them.

INVENTIONS

Romance in E flat

John Stench, newest man on the rodeo squad, looked right, then left, before adjusting the blue ascot beneath his chin. "What the blazes is going on here?" he exclaimed, rendering his pervert nag incapable. "I bought this dang thing to please Lisa, but all I get is a whirlwind of blade-dodging danger."

Larry Phillips, the boiler man from Petusa, ambled over. He wiped the swibble from his lips, leveled his chin four inches from Stench, and barked, "You'll never get that gal, John. She took off with Dog-Face Rhino two days ago. All you can hope for now is Stallion."

John shook his pony tail and tightened his saddle. "No use complaining, Larry. That girl won't listen. Every time I bring my homemade turnip soup to her shrivel on the prairie, she sits on her stoop and howls. No dog will go near her."

"Takes after her mother. Linguist, you know." Larry leaned on his empty foot, then added, "When the gravedigger threw dirt on her coffin, she pushed open the lid, shook her finger, and shouted, 'Don't you dare!' You don't see corpses like that around here anymore, that's for sure."

John pulled a squirter out of his pocket and shot protoliquid on his metatarsals and all three bunion cushions. "I won't try again, Larry. This is the last time you'll catch me with Heinrich Blieberhaft's Weltanschaung Plus. Lisa couldn't understand a word in that book, even though she's an Aramaic scholar."

Larry polished his glasses. "I wouldn't push book reading too far. Besides, scholars are for frying."

Both lads rose, grabbed their teething rings, tightened their diapers, and returned to their playpens.

GOD

Folk Dancing Is Transcendence in Action

The purpose of the art is to burn away the ego.

I returned to the Paramount last night at three a.m. after a beautiful evening of teaching folk dancing at Golden's Bridge—once again, folk dancing shows itself to be transcendence in action. When I told this to one of the dancers, she asked, "What is transcendence?" She looked like an educated person, so I thought she was kidding. But I could see by the vacant look in her eyes she was serious.

"Transcendence is going higher, going above," I said.

She walked away. How could an educated person not know what transcendence is? This word, this idea, which is so important to me, so central to my way of thinking, was, evidently, completely foreign to her. I wonder if it is to most folk dancers—to most people.

All those souls, dwelling in their transitory bodies, moving, flying, jumping, gliding across the floor in unison, listening to the rhythm and song from the Balkans, are unified by an unseen eternal vibration, the transcendent glue of a kabbalistic universe.

Joining Your Flow

I sat on my petal and contemplated the universe. Love and attachment crossed my mind. I dove into a plant, sizzled in ultimate union with an earthworm.

If this world is a miracle, what will the next one be like?

Beginning with nothing, my mind was soon filled with a plenitude of Emptiness, a vast harmonious vacuum. It raised me up, carried me skywards on eagle's wings, filled my heart with praise. I sat before the throne of the Great Illuminator, the Master Painter of the Sky. My eyes blinked with awe. Thunderstruck, I rolled across that sky—first leftward to plants, factories, and worm machines dominating the material landscape—and made obeisance to rules and heavy values of the terrestrial sphere; then I rolled right visiting the luminous emptiness of higher forms where the Absolute Thou Shalt Nots dwell, blazing under the Thou Shalt sun.

Tossed about, split by visions of right and left, I walked backwards to the Land of Inner Self. Deep within, treading the darkened caves of black wonder, I pondered paths of future and present being. Soon I emerged. I re-entering the day refreshed and inspired, hopeful my life would move beyond anxiety and its worship of vicissitudes to focus on a steady vision of the higher world.

Freedom from fear was my goal.

Words flowed, falling in buckets from heaven. Thankful and peaceful, I murmured, Flow on, flow on. Create an everlasting dam of mental protoplasm to hold the powerful rush of oncoming infinite thoughts. Come, white visions, roll, roll, roll. Lose me in your contradictory confines. I want to forget my tiny self that kicks and screams in its dreary valley, annoys my scattered parts, and calls forth nightmare obstacles laden with sin, guilt, earthly disasters, financial ruin, and endless worries about security. Free me from these stultifying black-vision phantoms of impotence. Such death-crow images do me absolutely no good. I need rolling thunder of the Great No, No! insisting I give up my Obstacle Vision, which creates icebergs of fear and mountains of disasters, forcing me to run for cover instead of attack the world.

I want Your Flow. It is my ticket to the fearless life, my connection to the higher forces ruling this changing, feckless, illusory world.

By writing, I join You. I want to pour words across the pages until I drop from exhaustion. Then I'll be simply too tired to worry about a thing. I'll fall on the floor in a happy pile. I'll lie face up, eyes on the ceiling but with inner vision fixed, far beyond, on the mountain peaks in Your Upper Realm where future words dwell.

Sanctify my efforts. Crucify me on the cross of Flow.

The antidote to pain is to work until exhaustion, until the pain itself is too tired to bother you.

Trapped within the confines of the known. I shrivel and wither in half-baked somnambulance; I crawl under the cool, shaded sun, sneaking wistful glances at the slow- flowing suburban river.

Why try? I'm hope to discover a hidden source of power located beyond the push, an America beyond America, one even Columbus never dreamed could exist; I want to find the City beyond cities, Land beyond lands, Realm beyond realms.

How else to rise from the imperfections of daily life?

The Ultimate Vision Guiding My Life

Do what you can for others, but do not forget your path; that is the ultimate message.

My path is not one of renunciation, but of action. Music is my center, purpose, and calling. It was revealed to me at age thirteen during the Cheerios Concerto, when I fell on the floor, weeping in wonder at the heroism and majesty of the Beethoven symphony I'd heard on the radio. That was the first door opening to a celestial vision beyond the temporal, spatial, earth, sun, public school, baseball, basketball, and everything important to the world of a child. God opened the door; a grand illumination entered, changing me forever.

My path was revealed: Remember that Vision. Bring it to others. That was all. Everything else became insignificant, a rest, a break from the true purpose. I call it a "vision," but it was actually a sound. Its brilliant white-hot particles covered the window glass, ceiling, and kitchen floor. My kitchen became my universe, vibrating, sparkling, dancing with a background of Milky Way, stars, and distant ethereal darkness.

My path, strewn with the mitzvahs of music, lay before me. There is my past and future life; nothing else to do but remember that vision and try fulfilling it.

Cheerios and the Ecstatic Experience

Ecstasy is the direct experience of God's power. It can be achieved through music or mitzvah. Mitzvah is ecstasy in action. Is there a moral quality to such ecstatic experience? No doubt. I feel the same emotional chills doing a mitzvah as I do listening to a Beethoven symphony.

One of my folk dance teaching goals is to bring my students such an ecstatic experience. My right foot dances in this world, while my left foot dances in the next. When I teach, I try to be in this world but not of it.

It is also the way I want to live.

Spiritual Practices

Can writing be a spiritual practice if I also want to be published? Can guitar playing be a spiritual practice if I still visualize the audience applauding?

My concerts are forms of service to higher and lower: Higher is my God walking around in a blue bathrobe in the corner of my mind; lower is the audience I hope to please.

I serve God and audience. I am slave to a dual master.

When someone likes my writing, a warm fluid of fullness floods my being: I love it! What can compare to love, understanding, and acceptance from my audience? Touching them is my orgasm beyond orgasms. I make love to them. I see my audience panting, reaching, craving me and only me. But beyond my physical body, they want my heart and mind as well. They understand even my spirit. I gladly give everything to them.

Then my audience melts into God Himself. He sits in front of me, leans back in His chair, listens, judges, accepts, and loves my performance. Before me I see His disguised body dressed as an audience of many. Each little head floats in the lake of Being.

I sit on stage, gazing out. Then I put my toe in the water.

Tennis into the 90s

Old men pinch their tennis rackets, flinging balls of fading fire into the cross-stitched nets. Sure they are heros for playing tennis way into their nineties. Is that where I am headed? Surely, yes. How the spirit fights as the body disintegrates. At first I admired their sagging bravery;

then I watched their bravery sagging. Focus not on the fickle penny-pinching, tight-assed skin of wandering youth, nor on the pappy-snatching, boil-marked skin of old age, but rather on the shiny lobsters clawing within, their hands filled with ripping fangs dripping red. These are the monsters that will kill time.

Mind holds all. But when it collapses, remember: We come from the divine; we live in the divine; we pass on to the divine; and through it all, we play tennis.

The Cheerios Experience: Witnessing the Divine Through Artistic Emotion

God bless Romaine Rolland! What a beautiful book he wrote in The Life of Ramakrishna. So many pregnant sentences and phrases that go straight to my heart. Some explain me better than I can explain myself. For example:

"Even in this first ecstasy (of Ramakrishna at six years old) the real character of the divine impress on the soul of this child can be seen. Artistic emotion, a passionate instinct for the beautiful was the first channel bringing him in contact with God. . . .the most immediate and natural with him was delight in the beautiful face of God which he saw in all that he looked upon. . . .The path of Ramakrishna is a far more dangerous one (than the rational path of Gandhi), but it leads further. . . . It is the way of love."

Artistic emotion, a passionate instinct for the beautiful, is truly my primary emotion and driving force. It was the channel through which I first witnessed the divine. My first meeting came during my Cheerios experience at age thirteen. I've had other meetings, too. Usually I am ashamed to admit this. I don't know why. Perhaps, rather than shame, it is a fear I will be laughed at or that, if I talk about it, the mystic experience itself will be diminished. It thrives in hidden fields of blinding light.

Paradoxically, when these fields are "brought to light," described, verbalized, often darkness descends upon them. At first I thought everybody had these experiences. But few seem to know what I'm talking about.

How important has this meeting been in my life?

Did it influence my decision to spend a year in southern France when I was nineteen?

Has it been the bulwark of my confidence, not only to travel, but to embark on precarious careers?

Did my stubbornness originate with this vision, so intense, so beautiful, that I won't give it up for anything because, without it, life is meaningless, and with it, infinitely rich and beautiful? It comes most often to me through music. I close my eyes and "hear" the divine.

Cheerios, Puritanism, Bar Mitzvah, and Beethoven

The Life of Ramakrishna, by Romaine Rolland, is such a rich, thick, juicy book I can only read a few sentences at a time. Sometimes I can do a paragraph. Then I have to spend several hours or days thinking about it. It is a bible, a spiritual description, not only of the life, mind, and thought of Ramakrishna, but of Indian philosophy as well.

How beautifully Ramakrishna unites the personal and impersonal aspects of God. How beautifully he points out the unity behind the apparent idolatry of worshiping the Mother Goddess, Kali.

"Kali is none other than he whom you call Brahman. Kali is Primitive Energy (Shakti)." To me, Primitive Energy means, among other things, sexual energy and the Kundalini serpent. How can I make my Kundalini serpent rise? Should I even bother? Why not just leave it lying on the lower level where it is? But whether on the low level or high level, the trick is seeing all Energy as the same. It is not a question of envisioning many levels but rather seeing all levels as part of the One.

Does that mean sex is neither good or bad? Aha! That old puritan question creeping in again. My puritanism started with my ancestors somewhere in biblical times. Yes, I'm responsible for my puritanical nature; I accept it. But I blame my ancestors for teaching it to me. It would be wonderful to be free of it. Years of psychoanalysis, therapy, walks around the block, reading, thinking, and countless other forms of self-exploration have not freed me.

Is this so bad? Maybe it's got some hidden wisdom of self-preservation in it. After all, part of me would just like to lie around and have sex all day. If I gave in to those urges, I'd end up a fetal ball of quasi-amorphous protoplasm. Perhaps my puritanism is forcing me into so- called "higher' thoughts, to channel my kundalini energy into longer-lasting forms like music, writing, running, dancing, business, even the stock market. I have a good instinct for self-preservation. Maybe puritanism is part of it.

Ramakrishna goes on: "When we call it (Shakti, Primitive Energy) inactive, we call it Brahman. But when it has the function of creating, preserving, or destroying, we call that Kali or Shakti. He who you call Brahman, she whom I call Kali, are no more different from each other than fire and its action of burning. If you think of the one, you automatically think of the other. To accept Kali is to accept Brahman. To accept Brahman is to accept Kali. Brahman and His power are identical."

This reminds me of kabbalistic writing. But writers on Indian philosophy are so much clearer! Perhaps that's why I am a Hinjew. Both Judaism and Hinduism are close to my heart.

"To Ramakrishna Maya itself was God, for everything was God. It too was one face of Brahman," says Rolland. Isn't this the Baal Shem Tov speaking?

Ramakrishna believes he can worship any god, since all gods lead to the same God. In the beginning we worship God through His physical incarnations, his avatars, Krishnas, Kalis, Jesuses, Allahs, Vishnus, etc.

Who then is my god? Beethoven, of course. Why not make Beethoven my avatar, the incarnation of my God? Throw in Mozart, too. Then add Tchaikovsky, Mendelssohn, Kazantzakis, Herman Hesse, and a few others I'll think of. These composers and writers have always been my gods. By focusing on my favorite, Beethoven, I will be worshiping one god. By adding the others, I'll be worshiping many. This polytheistic religion will bring me, through side roads, to the central monotheistic unity of Ramakrishna's vision.

Another quote from Rolland: "The Bhakta, whose knowledge is derived through love, begins by accepting one form of God as his chosen ideal, as Ramakrishna the Divine Mother. For a time he is absorbed in this one love. . . ."

I'm doing the same thing. Beethoven is my chosen form. (Perhaps he chose me, I'm not sure, but ultimately, it doesn't matter). I've worshipped him, along with Heifetz, Horowitz, Rubenstein, Milstein, Francescatti, Segovia, Bream, and other members of the artistic pantheon since I had my Cheerios vision at thirteen. They are my rabbis, priests, and gurus, the spiritual forms of my bar mitzvah, the foundation of my religious experience.

So I was bar mitzvahed after all! I had a Cheerios bar mitzvah with Beethoven conducting.

"There is nothing more corrupting than assured, lasting comfort" (Scott Nearing).

That is a quote I should swallow, digest, and send to every cell of my being. I should post it on lampshades, sing it in the morning, and plant it deep in the internal gardens of my rotating, up-and-down universe.

Scott Nearing's quote drains my desires.

Do I want to be wealthy? Suppose my dream came true and wealth rained down, making me financially secure forever. Would it cure sickness and death? Part of me would like some of the pain of too much wealth. But I know Nearing is right. Still, it's not the wealth that is the corrupter, but rather the vision of lasting comfort accompanied by a rejection of the grand effort. Death comes when trying stops and the impossible dream becomes a nightmare of lassitude.

With great wealth I could still follow the impossible dream. But I need not worry. I like to suffer too much. I like the pain of expanding starlight strewn across bloody stones. Jesus strumming the guitar on the cross is my hero.

King Mono, Beauty of the Universe

Concentrate: focus equals happiness. Concentrate on Beauty. In a secular age, people may not accept God, but they will accept Beauty. Mention God, and critics come out of the walls. Even I feel a bit uncomfortable using the word. Religion and religious language are not in my tradition. But Beauty is: Beauty is Truth, Truth Beauty, and both are synonyms for God. I have no problem talking about Beauty. My mother often said, "Oh, how beautiful!" I believed her. It's one of the exclamations she made that I agreed with wholeheartedly, one of her great contributions. I must thank her for giving me this most important justification for my feelings, verification of my most meaningful and unifying mystical and musical experience. Thank you, Ma, for opening up the world of Beauty, for ooing and aahing and growing tearful when you heard beautiful music. When I played the violin, you cooed and called it beautiful, too.

Beauty has been my highest melt-down experience. I have never been able to explain why. But that has never kept me from believing in its preeminence. Now, after reading religious and spiritual writers, studying mystics and their mystical experiences, I can see that my tears shed over the beauty of Beethoven correspond to their mystical unions with the Divine. They too broke down in tears, watched their egos dissolve, bathed in the wonder of a world created and controlled by the awesome power of King Mono, Beauty of the Universe.

It is the beginning and end of my search, the center of my being, what I search for when I teach folk dancing, write, play guitar, run, do yoga, or mingle in human relationships—all organized to create a space where Beauty may occur. My locations, stage sets, and scripts may be different. But their goal is always the same: to find King Mono, Beauty of the Universe, under a rock, behind a star, or beneath the sun.

October-December 1994

WRITING

Traveling in Depth

It's hard to write in my usual way this morning, so I'll have to write in an unusual way.

What is happening? I'm changing my routine. I'm starting the mornings with guitar, then song, then writing.

I keep discovering more and more on the guitar, better and better ways of playing. Yesterday, I dared relax my right wrist to the maximum. Voilà, the arpeggios in Villa-Lobos "Prelude Number 4" and the triplets of "Leyenda" both fell into place. This has never happened before. I took a daring leap forward and fell into the abyss of relaxation. I let go. A new world of guitar playing opened before me.

After the Solway Yoga and Folk Dance Weekend, I decided to start my mornings with guitar and follow them with singing. I sang the calypso song "Love, Love, Love" twice.

Then I realized I should practice all songs twice. Even better, work on one song a day: go over and over it, slowly, slowly, savoring, knowing, focusing on each vocal and guitar note. Travel in depth rather than laterally, moving down into the core, guts, essence of the song. Rediscover the universal vibration resonating in the center of its om.

Another decision I made was to take money out of the stock market and pay my debts. I've only lost money in the market. The best way for me to earn money is to work. I would make more money—or rather, lose less money, if I took all my money out of the market. But this kind of thinking, although sensible and rational, in no way motivates me to do anything.

I just knocked off two pages of writing. Play guitar, sing, then write. The whole process takes about two hours or more. Don't start running or yoga exercises until all three are done. Routine: Guitar, singing, writing, yoga exercises or running.

My Sea Is Not yet Dry

Bernice is on the phone with my grandson. I should talk to him; imagine, denying my son and grandson the opportunity of speaking with me just because I want time to write. How can I be such a cad? The answer is: not easily. But I shall try nevertheless. Cadhood is part of the price of writerhood.

I'll use any excuse to write, free my mind, and get the barrels of guilt off my back—to rid myself of the wailing wives, petulant mothers, endless obligations, musts and shoulds floating down the river in my direction—so that I can uncover my soul.

Mind gone askew. Ah, I love it! The mad dog barking in the universe, shooting the wild sound of grumbling guts into the Milky Way and beyond to burned-out stars and suns gone to seed. Metaphysical truths are hard to come by. They are born in elusive moments torn by knives, battering rams, and medieval maces. The doors of the universe do not open easily, but when they do, they swing slow and wide.

I'm roaring.

My sea is not yet dry.

Dr. Fok Dansz

Dr. Zoltan "Fok" Dansz is my alter ego. I'm writing his journal in the style of my New Leaf. Perhaps some day it and he will merge. Dr. Fok is off the wall; so are parts of my journal. He is a hidden voice in my New Leaf. He is me; I am him. Yet he is different. We'll see where he takes me.

The only thing missing from New Leaf is the emphasis on folk dancing. I almost never talk about the subject, but suppose I did? Would that make New Leaf kosher for him?

Comments of Dr. Zoltan "Fok" Dansz

I'm so excited about the publication of Folk Dancing Made Simple. This priceless work is beyond description. Hundreds have already purchased the cloth-bound edition. Advanced sales have my publishers, the Ujtanc Press, pressing in their pants. Many avid folk dancers have barricaded themselves inside the Ujtanc Building on Kerult utca; some have chained themselves to the doors. Nobody wants to leave without a copy of my book. Naturally, this makes me happy and proud.

Last night I taught Csárdás to the Cockpit at a Bat Mitzvah near the Dohanyi Street synogague. The young, middle aged, and old threw their hands high in the air with a magyar simcha. Afterwards, one of the dancers asked me: "Dr. Dansz, how did you inspire everyone to dance together even though many are so terrible at it?"

"Kérem, sir." I bowed humbly. "Please call me 'Fok.' Dr. Zoltan Dansz is my professional name. Only my publisher, the critics, and my wife call me that. To my friends I am simply 'Fok'."

"I'm not interested in your name or how you got it," said the man. "I am only interested in your teaching technique. How do you get this bunch all dancing on the same foot?"

I reflected a moment. Here was a serious aspirant in the art of the folk dance process. "Let me explain," I said. "From the moment I enter a room to teach folk dancing, my mind is totally concentrated on every person in that room, from the cripple sitting hunched and forgotten in the corner to the loud-mouth making jokes under the smoke clouds at the table on my right. I think about every one of them. Naturally, 'think' is not the proper word. One can only think of one thing at a time. That's why I call my method metathink, or unothink, because it transcends thinking. I use my higher faculties of intuition to see into the heart and soul of everybody in the room. That is my job. It mobilizes and occupies my mind. From my metathoughts come the mind and body movements, and the dance steps, that unite this room. People can sense what I am experiencing internally. It relaxes them, makes them feel accepted, quiets their fear of public humiliation on the dance floor. Once that fear is gone and they lose the terror of making mistakes, their dancing not only improves immediately, but with it the awkwardness of interacting with others disappears. A torrent of wonderful csárdás energy courses through their veins. They start going mad with dance, dancing 'like crazy.'"

"You've described it beautifully," said the man. "If I could verbalize like you, I'd become a professor."

"Words are good," I answered, "but I tried explaining the art of dance only because you asked me. In truth, it is best explained without words. The wordless song is the highest art form; all else is mere imitation. As the critic Baltimore Boniface said about Book II of *Folk Dance Made Simple*, 'It transcends language itself.'"

Although Book II has a period on page 64—a visual challenge for the reader—the rest is filled with blank pages, not only to emphasize the role of silence in deepening one's awareness of the cosmos, but to show how well wordlessness can teach a folk dance. For beneath wordlessness, in the human psyche, is still more wordlessness. Wordless levels wrapped in layers of awareness increase the further you descend. At the bottom rung of the ladder you find a vast lake of Nothingness, a vacuum filling the invisible waters and silent atmosphere. This bottomless realm is the home of metathink, energy center of the universe. I meditate on it before I teach dance; I remember it during my teaching. That is what made the sparks fly at this Bat Mitzvah—or any other event.

The Mere Factual Truth

Oh, how I hate facts! I am so bored with writing the mere factual truth about "what happened." Sitting on a pin makes you jump, and in jumping you rise higher, if not on the evolutionary ladder, at least on the corporeal. But writing mere facts, ugh! It makes me want to throw up!

Last night we saw the Tamburitzans from Duquesne University perform East European dances. What made it a great show? How does one write about such a concert? How to write about the transcendent forms given to man by the God of Folk Dance, who koloed, syrtosed, and horaed his way to health and wholeness in a biblical simcha before creating the world.

We're talking sparks here, dancing sparks.

Who Am I?

I am writing a secret journal. It is called the New Leaf Journal under the assumed name of Arany Janos. I am using the name for protection in case someone finds it; otherwise, I will be exposed for who I am.

Why should I care if others discover that?

Indeed a valid question, especially since I am not sure of the answer myself—suppose Zoltan Dansz is someone else? Would anybody know, or care?

Maybe I'm writing my journal because I can't answer these questions. Certainly to know oneself is a noble goal, some say the goal of life.

I used to believe my goal was to dance, and the more the better. Perhaps I was right. Perhaps my secret Uj Falevél (New Leaf) journal is my ego expressing its smaller self, while my larger self is expressed through dance. Intuitively I know this may be the case. Nevertheless, I privately yearn to attain the more common objectives—love, acceptance, respect, and pride, with touches of fame, grandiosity, immortality, and wealth thrown in. But I wouldn't want to express these desires in public. My image would suffer.

Am I my private or public self, or both, or someone else masquerading as a dance teacher? If I don't know, who would?

Since there is no other Dr. Fok as intuitive, intelligent, well-read, worldly, knowledgeable, or wise as I, I can consult no one else on these identity questions. The best person to ask is me. By writing my journal I ask myself these questions and try answering them, too.

I don't know others either, certainly not the dancers taking my classes. I teach them, talk to them, even join them for long, drawn-out philosophical and soul-searching lunches, but at the end of these intimate meetings, I'm no wiser. They probably don't know who I am either.

Maybe that's the nature of our short Budapest existence. I wonder if life is better in the smaller towns of Keckemét, Kalocsa, Mezökö-vesd, or Hódmezövásárhely.

Do people living near or among cows, trees, plants, and fresh air have a better sense of self? Or are they as lost as we are? Maybe they don't spend much time worrying about it.

Spinning Legs

A new day begins, and my legs are spinning in their sockets. Last night we grapevined in perfect step on the dance floor, creating a whirl of Greek steps that only islanders from Santorini, or their Atlantean ancestors, would appreciate. Zeus visited us. We undulated, fell on our knees, performed sweeping leg lifts, shimmied, and openly displaying our manliness before the surrounding women folk.

This morning my words are boiling like the stewed goulash I cooked on the Hortobagy plain when I collected swine-herd dances fourteen years ago. Ah, fourteen years ago. . . . I rode my csikos horse across the plain, scanning the horizon, checking out the sky laced with hora-swirling clouds; I searched with my sharp eyes for Christian monks playing volleyball and for the perfect peasant dance. I couldn't find it in the Hortobagy that year, but who cared? My purpose was to look. Besides, my horse was wild. Hortobagy wind blew through my hair as I inhaled the scent of distant hidden manure in the high grasses of this finale- flattened Eurasian steppe.

Suddenly, I heard the voice of my writing teacher, Ferenc Molnar, calling down to me from a star behind the Big Dipper. "Zoltan, don't do it! Stop this insane riding towards the fringes of your temperament. Wild Hortobagy horse riding can never tame your passions. Return to my class; explore the Hungarian word in its great ascending magyar cadence; create the definitive néptanc work. Write the bible of folk dance for your people. How wonderful to dissect proto-magyar roots and know the origins of words in everyday speech! When you teach us boot slapping in the powerful verbunk recruiting dance or csárdás from Mezőkövesd, you will convey our magyar national strength with even more magnificence. Remember when you danced ugrós and jumped through the roof? That was a great day on the dance floor."

I climbed off my horse and lay down on the grass in the middle of that vast and empty plain under the beauty of the shining sun. I agreed with Ferenc.

Certainly I would like to pen my terpsichorean vision, form a verbal mold filled with the vibrations of the myriad steps and patterns my restless feet have danced over the years. I would ask many questions: How did medieval Hungarian calves feel after dancing all night in a csárdá? Did they experience indigestion along with a longing for celestial visions?

At the Doors of a Great Harvest

I read my Greek and Turkish tour itineraries. They look good. Pages of history turned before my eyes. The white-washed walls of Suleiman the Magnificent before he toured the Ottoman Empire, the glassy bead-shining eyes of Mohammed after he conquered Constantinople in 1453. And what of Murad and Bayezid, great rulers, too. These squeaky names of empire builders slide within the narrow walls of my brain this evening as I sat before my computer, contemplating my next moves across Europe and the universe. Will folk dancing open up the world of history for me? Will Jan Hus, martyred in the Bohemian town of Tabor, make sense when I see him in the cool May light on Old Town Square above the cobblestones? And what of sailing to the Cyclades, Dodecanese, Sporades, even up the Greek coast itself, approaching the northern islands I have yet to see?

I mean to pluck the juicy names of history through folklore. These tools help me choose between the heroes of Greek mythology, pruning trees on Delos, oil spills on the north Aegean, or the movements of dancers going wild in third-century B.C. splendor.

I have opened a window into the language of the past. Sense meets nonsense on Ptolemaic shores as I hold septuagint hands in Alexandria. A door is opening.

I'm excited. Perhaps "why bother" is the first step towards rebirth. Suddenly, I see a way to write, not only about folk dancing, but about history as well. This means using the words of history: The names, places, dates, and geographies, all those loose tools lying scattered in the unorganized parts of my brain, may now step forward. My readings are grist for the writing mill! Greek words, Hebrew names, Hungarian clauses, Turkish agglutinations, Sumerian word roots, Finno-Ugric spellings, archeological digs, Hittite dynasties far from the shadows of Urartu and its modern Ararat spellings. Suddenly, anything goes as I catapult myself into a world of linguistic linguini perforated only by my plutocratic journal. New Leaf has matured into the Tree of Centuries. I have the key to its garden.

My tours and all their visceral, gut-wrenching experiences are bearing fruit—I am at the doors of a great harvest.

Writing Medication Relieves Depression

I just read an article in the New York Times about Tom Paxton (Joszef Feher). He had been depressed for years. Now he was on medication and "felt like slaying dragons." I don't know if he was kidding about the medication or not. Tom Paxton depressed? Why not? He joins a long list of artists who "suffer" from the illness.

Waking up slightly depressed is, for me, a common, everyday occurrence. My depressions do, of course, depress me, but they fascinate me, too. As I write about them, their black clouds slowly lift. Would I have written this morning if not for my depression? Do I want to go on medication like Tom Paxton? If I did, would I lose my creative source? Besides, I'm antimedication. I'd rather lie down and die in my depression hole than resort to "phony" medical supplements. It's part of who I am. I don't want to give it up.

It makes me unhappy to be depressed. But is happiness my goal in life, or productivity? I admire and respect treading the often-torturous creative path, the hero's path, on the way to higher things. Rather than accepting wimpish medication, I prefer to fight depression dragons in the open. That will make me tougher and wiser. By medicating them away, I am committing a crime against my creative self.

Besides, I have discovered my own medication: writing. Barry (Laszlo), my writing teacher, is the doctor in my medication program. His therapy is low-cost and productive. I have published three books and eight hundred pages of New Leaf journals to prove it.

The money depression excuse hit me again this week. I haven't worried about money for months. Suddenly, I've been hit by $2,000 in brochure and mailing costs, a $1,000 deposit for the spring Budapest/Prague tour, and $1,500 in estimated tax payments. The sudden decision to do a November mailing has thrown me. I hadn't even thought about it until I spoke with Arlene. I wanted to advertise my Old Greenwich, Connecticut, folk dance class opening January 13th; I wanted to send out my next Hungarian and Greek tour itineraries. Soon this desire grew into a November mailing. Expenses: Postage—$400; Arlene's addressing and packaging—$250; printing Hungarian and Greek fliers—$300; Bill Romano's computer setting of my mailing list—$150; $300 for Barbara Tapa's typesetting of the Folktrails Newsletter; another $600 for printing. Without blinking, I have added another $2,000 to my expenses. It will raise the level of my mailing from information to art. Barbara's graphics are beautiful. I don't mind paying for beauty. I do mind paying for some of Arlene's soupy, shitword writing with syrupy words like "sharing" and "communicate," the social work jargon of the politically correct world. I absolutely hate those words! Especially "sharing." I cut it out of the copy. I don't trust Arlene to write Newsletter copy, and yet I refuse to write it myself. Barry has suggested writing my own "column" for the newsletter. Perhaps someday I will. . . .

I can't stand the thought of medication for my depression. I want to fight this mental state, throw it off my back, learn from it. I won't medicate it away. My resistence is probably a macho thing. But what's wrong with being macho? Macho has gotten a bad rap lately, mostly from the women's movement, but we need some tough guys. Otherwise, who will protect the weak and defenseless?

Perhaps I shouldn't aim or even ask for happiness but find fulfillment through creativity. My medication writing program will release new forces. "Have you taken your medication yet, Jimmy boy?"

"Yes, Mommy. I've written for one hour."

I can increase medication by taking higher doses of history, folk dance, and language.

Crazy Sparks on Mount Sinai

I am hoping that, through the art of post-lunch-meal-on-the-brain writing, I will unearth sections of my historical unconscious, those words, events, and phrases so well loved and experienced during my college days.

Then I sat in my University of Rochester room gazing out the window, dreaming, not only of molecules and airborne particles floating on Genesee sunbeams before my eyes, but also about the physics of stars, light, and distant ever-receding universes filled with awe, wonder, and unanswerable questions. My goal was to touch the unfathomable mystery of the universe. Never mind the piddling tests, the stupid politics, the vapid social life on the fraternity quadrangle. The girls were great; the better part of them represented that unfathomable mystery of the universe.

Beautiful women, vibrations in fleshy forms, walking undulations of shine and glow—they were books without pages, oboes and clarinets emitting squeals of laughter, dynamos of poitrine protoplasmic sculpture.

That's why I want to write after lunch. I want to go beyond Moses, the burning bush, Sinai, and the commandments. Commandments and laws are necessary but they will not tell you why people should bother living together. That is found, not in laws, but in the crazy sparks.

What did Moses see beyond the commandments? Crazy sparks on Sinai.

Drug of Choice

Last night we watched the movie Tom Horn on TV. Good movie. But I woke up this morning drained and wasted. Watching TV steals my power. Almost anything is better, anything that keeps me in charge of my brains and lets me watch my thoughts float by. TV subtly steals my freedom. Its hypnotic fingers draw me close to the cesspool; slowly I sink into the viewing mode. Soon I am its prisoner, trapped by the images before me. When I finally emerge from this nightmare, I blink my eyes, quasi-throw up, look in the mirror, and ask my pale face, How did I get sucked into this?

If watching TV affects me so, imagine what it does to the whole country. Are other United States citizens also walking around in a TV-induced trance? Have the ubiquitous media also robbed them of their power?

How wonderful it feels to throw off the shackles of boobyhood, pick up a Vedanta philosophy by Vivekananda or Greek Made Easy book and use my own power again.

Watching TV is a subtle way of visiting the afterlife before your time has come. Worse: After death, the soul is even more active than the mind of the "live" TV viewer.

Nobody forces you to watch TV. If they did, it might be easier to say no.

Rather, the medium is simply placed in front of you. As images pass before your eyes, as the quiet hum of voice and sound lulls your brain into semi-somnolence, you become mesmerized. Your mind sinks into submission. TV is a finger of temptation calling you to begin your descent into the arms of the drug king Morpheus.

Ancient Mariner

Arrows of guilt are grazing my brain. "You'd better write, or else!" they say.

Their gentle push will soon turn into a hurricane in my solar plexus.

I'd better sit down at my computer and write something, write anything, to keep those doorstep demons away.

But a limbo state is a nothing state, a calm without peace. No wind. The sea is still. All I can do is wait. I long for demonic visits, for a wind to fill my sails and send my ship to the next harbor. I am the Ancient

Mariner becalmed at sea. Put an albatross around my neck, a pigeon, a sparrow—I need an imbalance to push me forward. I sit in my immobile ship. Is this the desireless state of yogis beyond passion and attachment?

There's no joy in stalling.

Joy comes when you fly with the wind. But here there is no wind, not even a breeze. I am in a state of high-class sleep. The inhabitants have gone away for the weekend.

Let not the pressure to write with meaning prevent me from writing whatever comes to mind.

Just because I've said everything doesn't mean I have to stop writing. Writing has little to do with having something to say. It has to do with writing, with placing one word after another.

The Tunnel of Perfection

What about working towards perfection? Do perfected writing and personhood go together? By perfecting the one, am I not perfecting the other?

When I think of the tunnel of perfection, I get claustrophobic. Could this fear simply be another mental game I play with myself, another illusion I create to make my world more interesting? Would it be dull without negative mental games—or would I create new, even better ones?

LANGUAGES

Intensity

Yesterday I wrote over eight pages—an hour in the morning, more before lunch, and a final batch in the late afternoon.

That's three times in one day. Moslems pray five times a day. Is there any religion besides Judaism that prays three times a day? Well, my own, the writing religion.

Today I feel really loose, and the words are dripping out like water from a leaking faucet. It's true of guitar, yoga, running, and dancing. The more I do them, the better they get. It's true about language study as well, and probably of just about anything.

I love languages and have been studying them since I started my Nép Utazás Travel Company. After touring Hungary, we ran tours on succeeding years to the Czech Republic, Moravia, Slovakia, Russia, Georgia, Armenia, the Ukraine, Israel, Egypt, Bulgaria, Turkey, Greece, Ireland, Spain, France, Germany, Sweden, Norway, Denmark, and Iceland.

To prepare for my tours to these countries, I took lessons in all their languages. First I studied the Slavic language family and learned Czech, Slovak, Russian, Ukrainian, and Bulgarian; then I moved to the Semitic languages, studying not only Hebrew and Arabic but also Babylonian, Phoenician, Canaanite, and Aramaic. I brushed against Armenian, Georgian, and Greek by putting in a few days of study—or was it months? I tried reading Homer, Aristotle, and the New Testament Greek.

Then I studied the Germanic languages to prepare for our tours to Germany, Iceland, Norway, and Sweden, and even studied a bit of Celtic for our tour to Ireland and Brittany.

I finished up with the agglutinative Finno-Ugric and Altaic families, studying Turkish, Finnish, Mongolian, and some Japanese.

Eventually I knew something about many languages but not one of them in depth.

So I decided to focus my efforts on Hebrew so I could read the Old Testament in the original.

"Ki?"

Picasso considered the destructive element the most important part of creativity. First comes destruction, then creation. First we clear the path of old trees, sod, worn-out plants, underbrush, and overgrowth. When all is clear, creativity flourishes by itself.

My duty every morning is therefore to clear the underbrush by pumping words across my pages. I am a faucet. How to turn myself on? Writing down the first thing that comes to mind is the first step.

Last night I dreamed about Kik azok, which means "Who are those?" in Hungarian. Ki az means "Who is this?"; Kik azok is the plural form.

Could kik or ki be related to the Latin quis or qui, and from there to the French qui, to the Germanic hwa, which became who in English? Is there a relationship, that is, between the Latin and the Indo-European languages, and a Finno-Ugric language like Hungarian?

If Hebrew is the foundation of all languages, what about hoo in Hebrew?

Who is the expert on languages? Ki, qui, hwa, hoo, who? Why not throw my opinions into the ring? Could the "Who is the expert?" be the Hebrew hoo, "(He) is the expert?" or even the Hebrew (She) hee being the "he" who is the "she" me? Is he hoo? Is who he? Or is he she? What about ki?

What if words like who, what, which, he, she, hoo, ki, qui, are all the same word? What if all pronouns come from the same root and are, in reality, the same word? If unity is the secret to everything, why shouldn't all language have originated from one?

Although not provable, this idea is plausible. I got it through deductive—or was it inductive?—reasoning. I'm not sure, because deductive and inductive are opposites, and opposites, being twins, cannot exist without each other.

On a higher level, opposites synthesize and become one. That's why he could be she, she could be he, this could be that, those could be these, which could be what, and tomorrow could be yesterday.

Similarities can break down into opposites, just as opposites can merge into similarities. This shows the world is One; differences and opposites are only superficial.

All languages may boil down to the same language; the fundamental root language may boil down to one word.

What would that word be?

Would it be The Word? The New Testament says: In the beginning was The Word.

I wonder if the word was ki?

Isaac Mozeson's "The Word"

Most of my linguistic life I have believed that a fundamental root language exists, and that this mythical language, called Indo-European by European (mostly Germanic 18th-and 19th-century) scholars, was originally spoken by a group of "proto-Europeans" living somewhere in Central Asia. Then, about four, five, or even ten thousand years ago—no one is quite sure—these Indo-European, Aryan people started migrating. Some moved south to India, where they pushed the original Dravidian population south. They became the ruling group, the priests and nobles, Brahmins and Kshatriyas (warriors). They brought their Aryan gods with them in the forms of Indra, Vishnu, Agni, etc.

Another group of Indo-Europeans migrated westward towards the Middle East and Europe, developing such language families as Latin, Germanic, Slavic, and subgroups like Greek, Armenian, etc. According to Indo-European scholars, Indo-European languages had no relationship to Semitic languages like Hebrew, ancient Phoenician, Canaanite, Babylonian, Akkadian, and, of course Sumerian, a whole other story. Sumerian might be related to modern Hungarian and the other languages in the Finno-Ugric group.

I believed these theories of language to be true. What else could I believe? Everyone I read, including my linguistic sound-change hero, Mario Pei, believed in the theory of Indo- European origins. When I started studying Hungarian about twelve years ago to coincide with my first tour of Hungary, my goal was not only to learn individual languages, but also families of them. I already knew something about Latin languages: French, Spanish, Portuguese, Italian, even Provencal, and I knew about the Germanic languages like English, German, Dutch, Swedish, Norwegian, and Icelandic (through the medieval Icelandic sagas of Snurri Sturluson; I liked the idea that Icelandic was close to the medieval Old Norse). I even approached Hungarian that way, researching, not only the origins of the Hungarians in Central Asia, but the Finno-Ugric groups of Finnish, and, moving to related agglutinative language groups such as Turkish—which I studied for my Turkish tour—and the Ural- Altaic group of Mongolian, and Japanese. When I studied Hebrew and Arabic, I thought in terms of the Semitic language group. I even delved into the Semitic languages of the ancient biblical peoples. There was no place for Hittite in any of these schemes, or modern Georgian or Basque, but I figured their origins might be discovered in the future. Thus, all my linguistic study has been based on family language roots in general, and word roots in particular—my approach to move from the particular to the general, to find relationships between words from different languages, to discover a unity in the myriad word forms of languages. It is an expression of my search for unity among the ever-changing forms in the universe. But I have yet to find it.

Therefore, what a shock it was to read that Hebrew is the root, not only of English, but of all Indo-European languages, and possibly of all languages! These are the theories of Isaac Mozeson and Rabbi Mattityaha Glazerson. Mozeson's book, The Word, is a twentieth- century classic. It traces the origins of hundreds of English words back to what he claims is their original Hebrew. I have been reading this "etymological dictionary" for almost two years now. First, I held it in my hands, only glancing through it occasionally. I was afraid to delve into it because I might end up believing what it said. This year, when I began reading the bible, I began reading The Word more seriously. The more I did, the more I discovered the Hebrew origins of English and other Indo-European languages, the more thrilled I became.

Could Mozeson be right? If I believed Hebrew to be the original tongue, this would be a major step, perhaps the major step, in my search for unity not only among languages, but between history and philosophy as well. I might even be able to tie Hungarian to Hebrew and who knows what else. The historic linguistic sound changes which took place as one people after another took over the Hebrew words, changing them to fit their speaking patterns, are, at first reading, simply unbelievable. But the more you read, the more believable they become. Relationships between words that you never thought existed, exist. The Word is linguistic "proof" of the Hebrew—English, Hebrew–Indo-European connection.

LIFE

Violations

God damn Aetna, my stupid insurance company, wants to cancel my car insurance. About a year ago, they sent me a letter raising my insurance because they claimed I had two violations: once I hit a car, and secondly, I ran a red light. I know I never hit a car. As for the red light, it's possible, but I don't remember it. That's two violations I believe I never committed. I called my insurance agent and told them to send me a copy of the violation to prove that it happened. After months of back and forth calls, neither Aetna, my insurance agent, nor perhaps even the police could find proof of any violation, and the charges were dropped. My car insurance continued as usual.

At that point I decided to change insurance agents. I didn't want this hassle again. Perhaps a new agent would fight for me better. Arlene recommended Derrick, so we changed to him.

About a month ago I get a letter from my Aetna agent saying my car insurance would be cancelled as of November 1. Why? Because of the two violations I had. These violations, which never existed in the first place, had supposedly been taken off the books six months ago. Now we were back to square one. Even worse, now they were cancelling me.

When I received this letter I immediately called Derrick, explained the situation to him, and told him to find me a new insurance policy. He said he would. When I called back yesterday, he said he doubted he could find me any insurance at all because of my "violations."

What good is this guy? I don't need another agent who is as miserable as the first. I need a fighter, someone who will go to bat for me so I don't have to waste my time doing it for myself. I'll have to go to bat for myself. That means wasting my time calling the insurance company, calling consumer groups to complain, calling agents, calling, calling, calling.

Fighting bureaucracy is something I absolutely hate. But I have little choice. If they take away my car insurance, eventually they will take away my driver's license and I'll be out of business. What a horrible mess. I can't stand this fucking bureaucracy and all the mistakes they keep making. And whenever I call them, all I get is answering tapes and electronic messages. I almost never reach a human being. If I do, they put me on hold.

I've tried approaching this with an attitude of yogic detachment. It hasn't worked a damn. The only way I'll reach that state of mind is by plunging into the process of fighting these miserable creeps, fighting the bureaucracy, fighting for my rights, and hopefully—this would be best of all—crushing these worms under my foot!

Two Essences

I've discovered the essence of life. Not bad for one day. Two essences, actually. First: Every moment is born fresh. Forget about "I've done this before; I've thought this before; I've experienced this before." These "before" attitudes exist only in my mind. In higher reality "before" does not exist. There is only the shining "now" dressed in the clothing of past, present, and future.

Love is the second essence. I discovered it teaching folk dancing at the Asarnow Bat Mitzvah. When I teach, I have an inner vision of all people before me. I push beyond the body–mind dual-ism and try to unite myself with everyone in the room. I push until my self dissolves. I achieve an egoless state. Some books I read call it Love. I do it whenever I teach, lead a tour, or run a weekend. I never thought of it as love. But perhaps it is I focus on the higher energy in the others surrounding me— Beethoven's Cheerios vision of oneness in action.

Numbers Are the Pole for My Genie

My ego is insatiable. Feed it and it only becomes hungrier. The only way to handle it is to dump it in the river. Easier said than done. That lousy bugger always returns to haunt and torture me. At least a fly or mosquito can be swatted, killed, and forgotten. But my ego always returns in myriad forms, in insidious disguises—as desire for a perfected body, an improved mind, an improved self, a need for respect and love, on and on.

We know its haunts; but how do you kill it?

My ego lives in the numbers when I count for the purpose of self-improvement. If I do forty push-ups, I'm average; sixty, I'm on my way; seventy, and I'm improving. I use these to transcend ego. But as long as I am counting, it will never disappear.

On the folk dance and yoga weekend, Rama told a story about a searcher, an aspirant who asked a yogi how to find enlightenment. The yogi answered: Meditate alone. The aspirant went to the mountains, settled in a cave, and began his meditations. One day, a genie appeared at the door of his cave. "I will give you anything you wish for," he said. The man wished, and every request was satisfied. Soon he ran out of requests. The genie said, "I have nothing to do. Give me work! Give me wishes to fulfill! If you don't, I'll eat you up!"

The terrified aspirant ran back to the yogi for advice. "My genie wants to eat me up," he cried. "What shall I do?"

"Tell the genie to climb up and down a pole," answered the yogi.

Baffled, the aspirant returned to his cave. When the genie appeared, he told him to climb up and down a pole. The genie fulfilled his wishes. He started climbing and never bothered the aspirant again.

In this story, the genie represents insatiable desire and endless movements of the mind; climbing up and down the pole, controlling the mind.

The power of mind has to be harnessed. Otherwise it will turn on you, eat you up, destroy you. Spiritual progress cannot be made without first asserting control over the mind.

When I focus on my interests, I am exerting mind control. Though

I am active, I am at peace. If my mind is not controlled, it usually sinks to a lower level, picking up self- destructive forces. That's why, when I have "nothing to do," I get nervous.

I know my mind is a loose cannon; it can shoot me or send me in a destructive direction. No wonder the resting periods after success or finishing a task disturb me. During them my mind is sitting poised, ready to pounce on me and eat me up. But when I count my push-ups, squats, or the number of times I play a piece, it helps focus my mind. Numbers are the pole for my genie.

Depression Revisited

I have to thank depression, my wake-up call. Without it I might never write a thing.

Why do I use the word "depression" to describe this prelude to the creative state? Partly because it feels like a heavy cloud hanging over my head that drains meaning and purpose from my life. Others often feel bad when you say you're depressed. But they should instead say, "Congratulations, Mr. Gold! I know your new depression will lead you to new galaxies. I envy you. I wish I could be depressed, too.

Alas, I'm just your average dullard doing the same thing every day. Once in awhile I change streets on my way to work. But I never get depressed! If I could, I might do something exciting with my life. Since I'm more interested in security than dynamism, though, I'm satisfied."

Without depression this page would not have been written. Depressions are God's reminders to stay on the path.

Marathon

Could my listlessness have started Sunday after watching the marathon on TV? Note that emphasis: Instead of running the marathon, I have been reduced to watching it on TV. Part of my summer program was to train for a marathon. That ended when my dance classes began.

Could it be that, when I started them, I gave up the dream of running a marathon? I need my dream. But how do I train for a marathon on a full work schedule?

Nothing Lasts

History has a way of washing over even the most monumental works and events of today. So why bother doing anything? Even suicide takes effort. Nothing lasts, though, not even that. It's just not worth the trouble.

Negative philosophies often give birth to positive ones. But my numbness is beyond opposites; it transcends polarity.

Speaking of numbness, there is something numbing in the nature of TV itself. Perhaps it's a combination of the medium's hypnotic effect and the low quality of most shows. No time to think, meditate, or argue. You just sit there absorbing whatever is thrown at you. Unlike a book, whose processing you can control, TV shows are pills in visual form. Ninety-eight percent of the medium is a total disaster and should be abolished. About ten years ago I read a book called Four Arguments Against Television. No one I know has read this book, yet it is most revolutionary. It claims that TV is a noxious medium, dangerous for both for physical and mental health. I agree.

But getting back to hopelessness—the only cure I have found is writing. I don't know why writing works, but it does. Downs are a necessary prelude to it; they bring wind-swept calls from Above. I am grateful to have discovered my own cure.

I am writing to save myself. Without its potent curative effect on my mind, I lose hope. Writing about Dr. Fok is off-beat and fun, but it is ultimately writing about him. It is not writing in him.

Maybe it should be. That's part of the Fok problem. I must write Dr. Fok for my survival. Otherwise, why bother? To write with the hope that someday others will read him is okay. But to write for my own survival, to lift the death-clouds that collect over my head, now that's a powerful reason.

I have never faced the personal importance of writing. It has been softened, disguised, window-dressed by the smaller meanings of public acceptance, publication, and hopes to please my readers. All are outer validations. But I have rarely, if ever, faced the gut- wrenching need to write, the public-be-damned, I-want-to-live, survival-of-my-soul method.

This is why Dr. Fok will never get far unless he merges with my New Leaf journal. I am looking for oneness.

I am moving slowly across the dance fields, taking a bath in the whirlpools of tourism. How shall I name them? The Zoltan Fok Dansz Tours, or Zoltan Tours? Does it matter? Mainly I want to collect a tourist herd and graze them across the glories of Hungary, my beautiful Magyarország. To dance with merry mustaches and wide aprons, sing songs from Debrecen, eat and drink, laugh, cry, visit porches, sit at dusk drinking bulls' blood while the sun sets over the plains or across the fur-fields laden with fruit wine, while we break our teeth speaking Hungarian. . . .

Zoltan, I am speaking to you. Reread your journals. Pick up all those old scraps of paper collected over years traveling the countryside, visiting the quilt-maker outside Pécs, or the laundress at Varalja, or clicking glasses with Miklos Koban at the csárda just below the mountain.

After eighty-six years it has finally happened: A lifetime of identity crises have fallen before my eyes. Always I have wondered, who am I? Am I Janos? Zoltan? Am I a Christian, a Jew, a Hindu, or all three? Am I a folk dance teacher or a hurdy-gurdy player/guitarist? I like to run the Budapest marathon. Am I a runner? I am also the vezetö (leader) and organizer of Nép Utazás (folk tours). Am I a tour organizer? All these identities dangle before me. The images of other haunt me too, especially late at night when I hide myself under the blankets and concentrate my mind on the oneness of the universe.

But today, I am happy to say, all my identities have merged. I have made my peace. Although all these are me, I have transcended them by merging them all into a higher unity. Bravo for me! My students sense my newfound strength. They love it.

The other day I was teaching my class in Uj Haven. It was another hot night and people were turning, jumping, and jiggling like crazy. I began to teach Baluca, Vlashki Tanc from Bulgaria. It's got an easy intro with lots of two-steps and walking; then come the fast crossing steps so typical of North Bulgarian dances, especially when the Vlachs do them. Somehow being so close to Romania makes Bulgarians love both off-beat and on-beat stamping. The class stood in a circle around me, and I launched into the first step. I was very concentrated as usual and started to dance without demonstrating or explaining. I often teach this way: Just do it! This time, I intuited that the students would know the dance even before I taught it. I communicated telepathically! Sure enough, once I started dancing they followed me easily, even doing the hard fast steps. The telepathic teaching continued all night. Although it was the first time I had taught that way, it didn't seem strange at all. Maybe I was on to something, a new didactic approach; or maybe it was something I had been doing unconsciously for years. Whatever it was, my teaching became stronger, my communicating skills more powerful, all without saying a word.

I plan to use the technique more in the future. How does it work? First, I concentrate on all the dancers; second, I visualize them dancing the steps I am about to teach; third, I dance, and everyone follows. Even though I can't explain the telepathic method any better than this, it works.

What about my interest in playing the classical and folk guitar Hungarian style? Franz Liszt was my idol when I grew up, even though he never wrote for guitar. I doubt he could even play one.

But that didn't matter. My parents were too poor for a large apartment, so a grand piano could never fit in; neither could an upright or a spinet. The only instruments that fit easily were a flute, violin, and guitar. I fell in love with the works of the nineteenth-century Spanish guitarist Francisco Tarrega, especially his haunting "Alhambra," so I bought a guitar and took lessons.

Now I serenade myself in my room at night. It is soothing, relaxing, and so elevating. Any worries I have about choreographies, dance steps, noisy students, or quarrelsome tour agents melt away as I pluck the strings of my classical guitar. I wonder if Tarrega had Hungarian blood in him—or maybe a Hungarian lover.

What about my interest in yoga and the yoga classics? Certainly the writings of Ramakrishna and Vivekananda prick my mind, even though neither ever visited Hungary. Vivekananda brought the vision of Ramakrishna to America at the turn of the century about the time I was born. When I was a child, my mother sat at my bedside before I went to sleep and read Vivekananda's writing on karma, jnana, and bhakti yoga as bed time stories.

New lives keep opening. Who cares if I am eighty-six (or is it eighty-seven?). Young, old, I am beyond old age and the fear of life or death—even thought my body will soon be going the way of the vipers and cats, and my mind will quickly follow. The eternal sun shines in the higher reaches of my mind. That is all I care about. I focus on the sun.

Laundromat of the Mind

I work to purify myself. Without doing so, I will quickly degenerate into a foul, disgusting soul wallowing in filth and blown about by black, destructive moods; my mind would hover above the sewer pits of Aquincum, that ancient ruin of a Roman spa on the outskirts of Budapest.

Luckily, though, I'm a professional. I can hide my weak, degenerate, and disgusting feelings quite well.

Also, I answer to a higher calling by trying to help my students. But can I really? The good ones are on their own road, doing their own laundry, cleaning out the miserable, degenerate, and disgusting aspects of their minds. I can only teach them Hungarian folk dance choreographies.

Is there a director of the Laundromat of the mind? And who does the choreography?

Whipsawed by the Creative Process

When we walked into Shira's bat mitzvah last night, I looked around and didn't see one person I knew. How peaceful this event is going to be, I thought. I don't have to talk to anyone. I can just observe and speak to my wife. We had a drink, some hors d'oeuvres, and waited for the room dividers to be removed.

I looked at the people present. All were soberly dressed, the men in dark suits, the women is print and formal dresses. A conservative, traditional crowd, very normal-looking and on the dull side.

When the dividers were taken down, we went to our table and met our table mates, pleasant couples from the New Jersey area. Then we settled down and waited for the uneventful evening to unfold.

On stage stood Tuvia, a one-man band from Israel. He played keyboard and sang Hebrew songs. Then he played an Israeli dance. Suddenly, all these boring people jumped up and started dancing the hora! They formed a circle, then several concentric circles. Their dancing got wilder and wilder. Smaller circles broke off. Some started improvising. Soon the crowd, which, a few moments before, had looked so boring, began to shout, scream, and dance like crazy. What a transformation! And this was only the beginning. As the night progressed, the dancing got even wilder. It became our best bat mitzvah in years. This morning, I got up feeling blue. I'd felt so good last night; why down this morning? Partly I was jealous of all those young dancers, lively, uninhibited, with unaching bodies that enabled them to jump up and down without warm-ups. But it was more than that: I felt the heaviness of creation, and the inevitability of dest-ruction, that is inherent in the creative process.

I create the world every morning when I wake up. I do it simply by opening my eyes. The world is a dream, my dream.

I am also its destroyer. On and on this cyclic process continues, rolling every hour, every day, for centuries, millennia. . .forever.

Down moods come during periods of destruction; up moods during creative ones. The downs leave me drained, hopeless, and forgotten. But just as surely, when I am down, a new burst of energy sweeps in to inspire me to create again. Such is the wedding. No doubt I would be "happier" if, instead of fighting my destructions, I accepted them as the inevitable part of the life process.

Work Conquers the "Why Bother?" Question

Why bother doing anything? I'll be dead soon; if not, then later.

So will all my friends and works. Successes and failures will be forgotten. Why do I listen to this voice? I don't know. Perhaps a better question is: How can I fight it? Even as I write, I feel the black cloud of ennui slowly rising. It is the nature of work to dispel this cloud. When I do anything, I slowly forget about the cloud. It returns only when I have time to question the purpose of my life and its meaning. I rarely get an answer to these questions. They seem a form of self-torture I like to inflict on myself. The same question of purpose keeps rising, and it remains unanswered until I get involved in some kind of work and forget about it.

Maybe I shouldn't even ask the questions. But that is impossible. The fear of death forces you to question the meaning of life. The only way to conquer that fear is by getting involved, working in something specific.

Thus I answer the "why bother?" question, not through words or thoughts, but through action. Even now I am feeling better. The act of writing has freed me.

Yoga

I discovered my power when I did the cobra. I bent backwards further than ever before. Wow, what a breakthrough! Then I remembered breakthroughs of the past. My superman complex had pushed me so far I ended up getting hurt.

I'm pulling back, taking a couple of days' rest.

Thanks, Ma, Thanks, Pa

Today is my mother's birthday. She is watching me from above, a perpetual presence sometimes standing directly before me, sometimes to the side, but always watching. She is my guardian angel, protecting me from many dangers and slips. Thanks, Ma.

She is watching my sore throat this morning. "Go to bed," she says. "Rest. Don't push yourself too hard. You may get sicker."

Thanks, Ma. But I don't want too much protection. I want offense as well as defense. I need a masculine approach to sickness as well as a feminine one.

The masculine approach comes from Pa. He's also watching over me, but from more of a distance. He's ready to step in but only in emergencies. He won't pay much attention to my sore throat. He's more interested in philosophy, religion, and abstract truths.

Ma takes care of my body; Pa deals with my soul.

Pa offers me perspective. I look at my sore throat as a passing phenomenon.

Pa also makes me think of the bible, Hebrew, and Elohim Himself. I remember when he told me about the philosophers before I went to college. I was seventeen. How wonderful to learn that higher ideas existed and that philosophers over the centuries had given them countless hours of thought.

That Is My Job

Success is as big a distraction as failure. I'm talking about my attitude of attachment to success and failure. That's the killer, attachment.

I long for tour registrants, money, larger folk dance classes, weekend registrants, etc. Now suddenly, I have more registrants than ever. New potentials are calling or writing almost every day. It is not an avalanche but feels like one.

Yesterday I was traumatized by the sudden rash of calls, letters, and actual tour deposits. How do I handle this success? Will it put more pressure on me than failure? Will it last? Am I happier with it?

Karma yoga says: Work but do not become attached to the fruits of your labor. I want to dedicate my labor to the Silent One in my higher nature.

"The Company of People Who Don't Exist"

William Trevor spends a good part of each day writing. "I get melancholy if I don't," he explained. "I need the company of people who don't exist—they keep me going."

I like that. I need company too—my printed word reminding me of who, where, and why I am. I've felt this ever since I gave up the violin. Although that king of instruments put me in touch with the sun, stars, and most powerful of celestial forces, it was not enough. Creating was even better.

The High School of Music and Art introduced me to music and the epiphany of sound. College introduced me to the beauty and magic of the printed word. Once I started reading about ideas, I knew music alone wasn't enough. I needed music, ideas, and language. I went to France, studied French, played guitar, sang, then took a room in Greenwich Village to spend three years writing. It was the beginning of a thirty-year experiment to find the source of my creativity and the reason I passed through states of melancholy. Why should this be, when music and the presence of others lifted me so high? Did it point to an aspect of me I didn't quite know yet?

I don't need the company of people who don't exist to keep me going. I need the company of myself, my real self, a self that often gets lost or forgotten as I tramp through the world of weights, letters, raucous sounds, expenses, and social pressures.

I discovered journal writing. It is the ultimate whirlwind of my soul bursting free from its fetters, driving through lanes and byways, past scattered clouds and rumbling brooks, beneath the lighting flashes and burst of thunder, carrying a word-hurrying blitz of ever- friendly verbal constellations. I am lucky to be an instrument strummed and plucked by One whose delicate hands, strung with fingers of shining steel, whirl through every capillary, creating tonal monuments.

Witness

I did the witness exercise while running—visualized my "self" floating just outside my body, above my head. I became my own witness. What perspective it gave me! But I ended up with a headache because, even though I realized the truth of the experience, I did not want to give up my old beliefs and my way of life. By stepping outside myself and "witnessing" myself, I was experiencing the eternal. A heady experience, yes, but tinged with anger and loneliness. I was not ready to give up my passions, hopes, loves, fears, and desires. How could I drop everything and follow the Higher Path? Yet I knew it was the path of truth and freedom from fear.

Of Power and Many Lives

Why should I try to accomplish everything during this life alone? It puts unrealistic pressure on me and vitiates my power. By trying to fulfill all my dreams in this brief compass, I am setting myself up for frustration, impotence, and failure. There is no reason why I should live with such negatives. Rather than take the short-term, one-life view, take the long-term, many-life one. Accomplish things slowly, over centuries. I may not have all day, but I do have forever. Standing under the sun of many-lives drains away any reason to rush towards immediate victories or dwell on short-term defeats.

During this life I have put myself on the language path, the leadership path, the music, dance, history, yoga, and running paths. Perhaps these started in former lives. No doubt talents from former lives come easily to me now, just as unsolved problems from the past pursue me into this life. My rush to accomplishment is caused by lack of long-range perspective.

Revisiting Mom

My lower back tightens.

The library of ancient fears protects me from the hand of the Giant Mother, Goddess of Illusion, Metaphysical Mom who stands ready to strike me down whenever I stand up. Who could this be but beloved protector, defender, and communist menace of my childhood? She is busy defending me against myself, against the freedom rising up within me. Under the aegis of the Giant Goddess I can remain her slave, receiving love in the form of kisses, smiles, and suffocation.

It is time to revisit Mom and the dancing devils stamping on my malleable childhood brain, filling it with illusions about who I am supposed to be but not about who I am.

Revisiting Mom: I spoke up to her only once, and she slapped the shit out of me. I'm a fast learner. This was not the way to go. So I stopped speaking up, internalizing my rebellion. Today I speak but am cursed by not believing in my strength. Using short kicks from Vivekananda and other high fliers, however, I'm going to change that.

Good-bye goblins of the slapping hand. I'm sick of seeing your disgusting, ever-present, pernicious faces. You're going down the drain with my morning shower water. I don't know how, why, or where, but you are going! No more living with ghosts and creeps who make me miserable. You've had a free ride in my house for too long.

Good-bye, monsters. You have become a cloud.

Vivekananda

I would love to think that Judaism, kabbala, gematria, Hebrew, the Tannach, all of Jewish writings and culture, have answers above and beyond the writings of non-Jews. It touches my sense of Jewish nationalism. Imagine being part of the elite chosen by God Himself to be better than everyone else. Of course, I know that the chosen people were chosen to bring the moral teachings of the Torah to others. I'm not interested in that today but rather in the hubris part. This morning I just feel like being better than anyone else. I wish Judaism would fulfill that need for me, but it doesn't. In fact, the writings of Vivekananda about Vedanta are better than most Jewish writings I have ever read. Vivekananda was not Jewish, but he was a universalist. So were the wisest of the Jews. They, like he, didn't waste their time thinking about being better than others. Rather, they focused on their relationship to God, and from God to man, universality, peace, and oneness.

MONEY AND ITS BRETHREN

You Do Your Job, I'll Do Mine

The phone just rang: an inquiry about our Yoga and Folk Dance Weekend. Although the guy who called is from Waldwick and no one has ever come on a weekend from Waldwick, I still gave him a sales pitch, sent him a brochure, and hope he'll register as the first to break the Waldwick non-registration record.

Paul Laifer called yesterday and gave me the prices for the Israel tour.

I'll have to send him $4,000, and that will clean out my account. Of course, the money wasn't mine to begin with, but I've held it so long it feels like mine.

I'm quickly moving back to an empty checkbook. Nothing new here, just a return of the ever-recurring nightmare of financial ruin and disaster.

The fear of financial ruin has the same feel as the depression I experienced earlier this morning—a passing cloud in my sky, a nail hammering on my head, but one that could disappear in a moment. In fact, it disappeared after that the guy from Waldwick called.

Money, along with everything else, comes from God. Maybe He is setting up the financial disaster nightmare as an obstacle to overcome so I can learn about Him, faith, and His higher forces. He's trying to teach me something. I just don't get it yet. "Hey, Jim," He says. "I'll send you money when you need it. Stop worrying. Money and registrations are my job. They are not in your hands. Learn how to delegate. Your job is to work and love me. I'll take care of the rest. You do your job, I'll do mine."

Stock Market Dilemma

Should I sell all my stocks?
Since I have gotten into the stock market I have only lost money.

True, I've played with small stocks, and therein are most of my losses. But the question is: what should I do?

In the past the answer would have been: nothing. Just wait it out and hope my situation will change.

Why did God put me into the market? What am I supposed to learn from all these losses, these market frustrations? I know I've been going to college, the University of Financial Losses, and must pay my tuition. Am I ready to graduate?

Well, first of all, why am I addicted to the game? It is a game of hope. Whenever my stocks go up, I decide to stay; when they go down, I decide to leave. I've been whipsawed so often that at this point, I simply can't decide at all. Frozen. Immobile. Stuck. Is the best decision no decision at all? What a dilemma.

PERFORMANCE

Singing, Hyperventilation, and "Turiya"

I'm at Solway's in Hillside 1, a great room. We should always take this room.

This morning I suddenly understood the Hebrew hifil verbs, especially the present tense. I used hitchil—to begin—and conjugated it with ani matchil,ata matchil, who matchil, anachnu matchilim, and, anachnu matchilot, etc.

"When you are ready, your teacher will appear." Months, even years of study with little comprehension—then, suddenly, one day, there is a clearing; the sun shines: I understand. Plant the seed, water the garden, soon a flower will grow. The only question is: when?

I hyperventilated when I sang this morning. After "Mule Skinner Blues," "Cucurucuci," and "Malaguena Salerosa," I felt dizzy and almost fell unconsciousness on the floor. I know this is due to hyperventilation. I lay down on the bed, had a nice sleep, then awoke suddenly with quick short breaths. It felt like panic.

Suppose my singing is related to yogic breathing, pranayama? Suppose almost losing consciousness is really a positive experience, a first step into turiya, the state beyond consciousness and unconsciousness, even beyond deep sleep? According to yoga philosophy there are four states of consciousness: consciousness, unconsciousness and the dream state, deep sleep, and turiya, the state of unity beyond deep sleep where one is "conscious" of oneness. This state is impossible to describe in words. It is beyond language. Nevertheless, it can be experienced. Perhaps my singing is the doorway to turiya. What an idea!

Why the panic at the end of the rapid breathing? Perhaps it signals the energizing and reawakening of my ego and its re-entry into this material world. Very interesting. . . .

Thinking of the Audience

I just want to get those fast fingers flying.

Fast, indeed. And not too many ideas behind them. I'm aiming to inhabit that vast Vacuum in the Sky.

I'm avoiding the main idea of the morning, too. But that's okay. It's too big to talk about, anyway, too good an idea to open up to analytical fireworks.

And yet to play guitar with only the audience in mind, to practice in the privacy of my own home, not only guitar and singing, but writing and yoga with only the audience in mind, is an incredible leap beyond ego into the land of the selfless. Finally, after decades of questions about how to handle an audience, I now conclude, after reading Vivekananda on karma yoga, that the answer is: Think only of the audience. Of course, that's perfection; I'm not close to it. But I'll be approaching it for the rest of my life—for what is perfection but peace, bliss, and end to conflict, and this is impossible to achieve permanently while still living.

We work to forget, to purify, ourselves.

Imagine focusing in this way: every thought creating waves that reverberate through the universe, not for hours, days, or months, but for years, generations, and centuries! If it takes light traveling from a distant star thousands of years to affect anyone on earth, why shouldn't the same be true for my thought waves? Or yours?

This shows not only the incredible power of thought but also the importance of all my thoughts. Playing guitar in the lamplit corner of my room affects someone in Mongolia or even someone living two thousand years from now in Alaska.

Who cares whether these people pick up my vibrations today or next century? When is not as important as how and why.

The Birth of Danceobabble

I mounted the thirty-two wooden steps to my top floor, mirror-lined dance studio at 6 Gyarmat utca. But I was in no mood to practice dancing.

I am rarely in a dancing mood when I enter my studio. Perhaps Gyarmat utca is too far from the Danube, or the studio is too dark, or I need live music, or I crave the hot blood of an audience or even the worldly inspiration of cash payment. Whatever the reason, I'm rarely in a dancing the mood when I enter my studio.

Yet dance I must. Not only Hungarian repertoire, but dances from Bulgaria, Macedonia, Greece, Romania, Turkey, Israel, Serbia, Slovakia, Russian, Ukraine, France, and the Netherlands as well.

First I warm up with some unorthodox improvisations, gently shaking my shoulders, grinding my teeth, waddling like a duck in half-squat position, and barking out Old Testament phrases in Hebrew and Hungarian. Like dancing itself, my improvisations are beyond language. I have a "secret" language to "describe" my warm-ups: It is called danceobabble, the language of improvisation. It wipes the cobwebs from the mind so that the throbbings of the heart may shine pure and clear.

How do I transcribe danceobabble to the printed page?

I place a keyboard under my dance floor with a thin piece of wire attached to each key. Then I turn on my computer screen and begin to dance. Danceobabble words and phrases appear on the screen. Thus I can write a journal while I dance.

Hungarian Fiddle Farm

This morning I applied for a government license to open the first Hungarian Folk Fiddle Farm, where we will train the future Hungarian violinists. Fiddlers are losing work since communism fell. We must insure their musical future.

My Fiddle Farm has a grand design. I see musicians playing concertos in fields, garages, smith shops, and barns. Our farm will also take in the fiddle bums I see loitering around the Danube. These beggars with cups hanging from their violins not only ruin our tourist trade but miss hundreds of notes in their pathetic renditions of the so-called Hungarian classics. Imagine playing Liszt on a two-string violin or Bartok standing knee-deep in a garbage can. These tricks only debase our music. Instead of destroying their performances, beggars can teach at my Fiddle Farm and get a good meal and bath, too.

Once the farm is established, I plan to hire teachers of hegedü (violin), kontra (viola), bögö (double bass), duda (bagpipe), cimbalom, and even the tekerölant (hurdy-gurdy). Along with administering the farm I will also teach the most important Hungarian dances including csárdás, verbunk, körtanc, ugrós, and legenyes.

Career

Clouds of Sunday morning sadness are descending upon me. What causes this? The sky? Vapors rising from the Danube?

It is so hard to know the reasons for my mood swings. It might have something to do with what my Judka said to me last night after she spilled her goulash in my lap. I screamed, hopped on one foot, shouting, "My feet, my feet!" I thought my career in dancing was finished.

She replied, "Zoltan, shut up!"

I was flabbergasted. What about sympathy? What about compassion and love? What about apologizing? All she could do was blame me for placing my lap under her boiling goulash. "Be more careful, and nothing will happen to you," she said.

First I thought, She's blaming the victim. But then I reconsidered. My wife is very wise. Although I can't stand most of her reactions, she's often right. Besides, I would be better off making myself responsible for accidents that happen to me. It would give me more power— and I love power!

As the skin on my foot peeled under the boiling goulash and I hopped to the freezer to lay my hand on an ice pack, I also realized this accident might be a good thing. I had years of training in the University of Szeged Dance Department of Magyar Néptanc, years spent building up dance contacts in performing companies from Jászberény to Niregyháza to Debrecen to Sárospatak, Sátoralyaújhely, Mátészalka, Szombathely, Sopron, Szekszárd, Kalocsa, Hajdúszoboszló, Pécs, and Kecskemét—where I convinced Zoltán Kodály to arrange a peasant folk tune for our dance company. Even so, some physical or mental catastrophe could easily end my career.

How good was it to be so attached? What kind of freedom can come from that? None at all. Attachment to Judka, career, or anything else could only lead to a higher form of slavery. How could I free myself from my chains, work in freedom, and continue to love? If this were possible I would be able to love my wife, my work, and even Ferenc's miserable bagpipe playing.

Last night I taught etvorka, my favorite Macedonian dance. To my amazement, everybody got it—and these were beginners.

This morning I met Laszlo Kovacs, president of Ujtanc Press. He pressured me to finish Hungarian Folk Dancing. I have been writing it for twenty years. Somehow there is always more research to do, another village to visit, new manuscripts turning up in the Budapest Ethnographic Museum Library, recently discovered sites of Proto-Hungarians in Turkey, Iraq, and Mongolia. As a result, I have only completed six pages of the manuscript. Laszlo is not impressed. Twenty years for six pages isn't much.

What is preventing me from telling the story of my folk dancing?

Take etvorka: et means "four" in Macedonian, and vorka means "times"; so etvorka means "four times." I can easily write about technical terms, the structure of the dance, the meaning of its name. But I can't write about its essence. I must wait for divine guidance.

Cappuccino Was the Culprit

Last night Judka and I were sitting in the Hungarian Café on Rákóczi útca with our friends, the well-known water colorist from Pécs Gustave Nagymarosy and his wife Maria, a potter and health professional from Debrecen.

While we were talking about such artistic topics as diabetes, arthritis, the effect of vitamins on the nervous system, brain tumors, health, and dying, I ordered my second cup of cappuccino.

As I sipped it, suddenly I felt a pain in my eye. At first I thought a mosquito or fly had flown in. I pulled my top eyelid over my bottom one to remove it. No luck. My eye began to hurt. When I went home and looked in the mirror, I saw that a blood vessel had burst.

Why had this happened? Was it the subjects of our conversation? The cappuccino? Pretzels? Why does one get sick in the first place?

Judka suggested I take vitamin C to strengthen my blood vessels. I decided to cut back on caffeine. I suspected my broken blood vessel had something to do with the cappuccino. I had felt something break inside my eye as I drank it. I've read that cappuccino can break a blood vessel but always thought moderation would save me.

But my moderation had diminished over in the past few months as I added more cappuccino to my diet, along with new cakes, cookies, halvah, pastries at the Kecskemét bake shop, and Chinese sesame bars, which I found at the newspaper kiosk on the Andrássy útca.

I hate to admit that a healthy folk dance teacher can be frightened by the breaking of a blood vessel. Fear flooded my being, and my confidence fell below zero. What had happened to my Hungarian macho? Today I am recovered—but the question remains: Can I trust my instincts? If I believe them, then I know that the blood vessel broke because of the cappuccino! Can I prove this? No. But if I am to believe in listening to my inner instinctual voice, it told me cappuccino was the culprit.

An American Folk Dance Citizen

Zoltan Fok Dansz has moved his base to America. A Hungarian-American with dual citizenship, dancing with one foot in Budapest and the other in New York, he takes a job teaching folk dancing in New Haven, Connecticut; Englewood, New Jersey; and Riverdale, New York. He becomes part of the New York-area Eastern folk dance scene. His arrival is met with huge crowds of dancers who want to learn new dances. There are not many eighty- six-year-old teachers left, especially ones who can still dance with the flair and paprikas fervor of a Zoltan Fok Dansz. His classes quickly fill with enthusiasts. Everyone wants to know the secret of the long and active life he embodies. Just as Vivekananda came to America at the turn of the twentieth century to bring the teachings of Ramakrishna to the west, so Zoltan Fok Dansz feels that America will be receptive to his message.

Friday Nights

I've merged Zoltan Fok Dansz with Jim Gold. Now I can go back to the fluid writings I love, to the bible, beyond time and space. I can lose myself in the uncoagulated universe where plot and pasture never mingle; I am back to the free form of undiscovered land- locked writings where biblical cranes fly overhead and cooked peas of the new age bristle in their home-green pods.

My lover is a word. Her friends are words, too. I love her friends. Her boss, the Big Lover, is the Word.

The sound of words haunts my being; they bring sweet vibrations from the Void. My fingers are flying again. That's the way it should be.

What a thrill to read the Old Testament in the original Hebrew! All those years of study are paying off.

Where is Zoltan this morning? Hiding in the bathroom, no doubt. "Zoltan, Zoltan, come out! Get off the pot and start writing. I miss you!"

I'm sitting in Branford, Connecticut, writing in the lovely Weissian Room. It has two windows; one faces the barren November woods, the other a quiet street. Sunlight streams in. Coming to New Haven twice a month may well be my personal vacation, especially when I can use Saturday morning to write in the Weissian Room. Slowly my decision is being made.

I may keep both New Haven and Greenwich groups. Dance four Fridays a month in Connecticut? Two locations? We'll see. I'll know more the end of February. But now I'm more relaxed in New Haven. Wouldn't it be funny if the long ride up proved a blessing in disguise, though I couldn't do it without the sleep-over at the Weisses.

This means I would be going to New Haven for its "vacation aspect." Plus the group is young, dynamic, and a pleasure to teach. I love the work.

I may end up even liking the commute. If I add Greenwich and keep New Haven, I'll be teaching every Friday night. Will I like that? What else would be more fun than teaching such good dancers? If this is true, then doing it every Friday night would be a fine weekend activity for me—my weekend coffee shop on wheels, a gathering of friends for a good time. Judka could join us in Greenwich. She wants to folk dance on Friday nights. Now her wishes can come true. The more I think about it, the better it gets.

Actually, I don't have much to think about. Folk Dance Fridays in Connecticut are a great idea. Having two locations is even better; one group can feed another.

As for the rest of my activities, I'll just keep doing them as is. The income from my new Friday night groups might make up for my losses on folk dance weekends; the groups also may bring new customers for my tours.

But I don't need secondary reasons for running my Friday night groups. I'll run them primarily because Friday night folk dancing is fun!

I am thinking through the guitar!

I first saw Alexander Bellow do it in a concert twenty-five years ago, and I've always remembered it. Bellow wasn't a good guitarist, and the music he played, mostly his own compositions, was really terrible. But while he performed before an intimate audience in a school auditorium in Clifton, New Jersey, I could hear him thinking on the guitar as he played. I had never heard anyone do that. The experience stayed in my mind as a wonderful way to play.

In the past I tried to imitate the Segovias, Julian Breams, Rey de la Torreses, and Sabicases. But now the need to fulfill someone else's vision has fallen away.

Expanding My Audience

What good are all my music skills if I never use them publically? Is it selfish to keep your talents only for yourself?

I need, nevertheless, to give up public performances. This does not mean I will give up private performances, though who will listen to them? God and the universe. Alone in my room, playing guitar, I send vibrations throughout the universe, to past, present, and future souls, and the Great Soul Himself.

So, paradoxically, by giving up public performances, I am expanding my audience; I am no longer limited to those I can see. My listeners have become an ethereal collection of souls beyond the restrictions of time and space.

My Polyphonic Stew

For years I have been trying to put my performing in boxes: folk song box, classical guitar, flamencan guitar, writing, and readings.

None of these boxes work. I can give a one-box show in the privacy of my own home, but as soon as I walk out on stage to face a live audience, I jump out of my boxes. I draw on every skill, both spontaneous and practiced, to milk the moment. I am forced to turn stage performance into a creative act never done before and never repeatable.

The essence of my performance is to create something new on the spot. Songs, stories, classical guitar, audience participation songs, and ad libs are bricks I use to build my house on stage. Hopefully, I am improving real estate values.

New Year's Resolution/Revolution

Classic guitar is my form of private prayer.

In public, my talent lies, not in performing private guitar prayers, but in displaying my mouth. I know how to talk and kibbitz.

It's a talent. I may prefer others, but that's the one I've got. I know facts, but when they come out of my mouth something happens to them—they emerge in another form.

That's the way my concerts go. Good or bad, I must go with my instincts.

It all fell into place last night.

I started my program by reading "Depressions Can Be Fun" from my Crusader Tours. Then I sang "Palace of the Czar" and "Moscow Nights" in five "L" languages. Excellent openers. This was followed by Long Island Yodel. Then I played the three-fourths beauty, "Tumbalalaika"; next came "Love, Love, Love." By then I was warmed up and on my way.

When I played four renaissance dances on the classical guitar, I knew I was in trouble. I shortened the four dances to one, following it with Granados's "Spanish Dance Number Five," which I shortened to half. I sweated through these pieces, knowing they were "wrong"; I was "using them" to prove myself to the audience. Then I realized this was my last public performance on the classical guitar. My public torment and suffering were over.

Free at last! I want to glow a bit longer. Free, free, free! Luxuriate in my new state. I want to dance down the street for joy.

Guitar

I start guitar practice by warming up with the same exercises every day. I begin with ligatos, then play C and G scale patterns up and down the neck. Then I relax my right hand by playing my Bellow's arpeggios. These warm-up exercises take about fifteen minutes; they are automatic, easy, soothing, and relaxing. When I am finished, I am in the mood to play guitar.

Thinking on the Guitar

I met with Mr. Afternoon when I played my guitar after lunch.

I began with Fernando Sor's "Sonata in C," playing it slowly and softly, not wanting to pull a finger muscle. I played right away—without warming up. Well, not actually played. I thought on the guitar.

I listened carefully to every tone and note.

In the process, I discovered sound within sound, notes within notes, phrases within phrases, worlds behind worlds, and worlds within worlds. I felt like the prophet Ezekiel discovering wheels within wheels.

I thought on the guitar!

BUSINESS

Dreams

I have fulfilled my dreams: My dream of organizing tours to thirteen different countries in Europe, Eastern Europe, and the Middle East has reached its end. It didn't turn out exactly the way I had planned. I dreamed of running a large company, with tours to Norway, Sweden, Denmark, Iceland, France, Spain, Italy, Czechoslovakia, Bulgaria, Romania, Hungary, Yugoslavia, Greece, Turkey, Poland, the then Soviet Union, Israel, Egypt, Ireland, England, and perhaps Morocco. I've run tours to many of those countries, but my tour dream has diminished in design from a large company to a one-man show. Nevertheless, the core of the dream has been accomplished: I have developed tour-leader and folk dance- teaching skills. Tours are still fun but not in the same way they were when I started. Most of the anxiety is gone, and so is the excitement. Evidently, without anxiety I can't have excitement.

There's not much anxiety or excitement in running weekends and folk dance classes either. Sure, they are fun and I like them, but the high-level of fear, worry, and trembling I used to experience is largely gone.

I once had hopes of being a successful writer. How excited I was when Mad Shoes was published seven years ago. It felt like the highlight of my life! Since then, it's been downhill on the excitement road. With the publication of Crusader Tours, my desire to publish has fallen to zero.

Once upon a time, I gave concerts. They made me nervous enough. That went on for years. Now that I've "conquered" the guitar and reached my goal of playing the "Alhambra," I've stopped giving concerts. Concerts are the only remaining thing that might make me nervous. Does that mean there is some excitement left in them, that I should go back to concerts? But I'm too lazy to pursue bookings. I want to write, study, meditate, and play guitar. Some day I may return to concerts. Then we'll see if they still make me nervous.

Last night when I heard a tape of my guitar playing, it sounded beautiful. And this was a bad tape! I'll tape all my guitar pieces and songs. But this kind of project does not get me nervous or excited. It is more a gathering of things I have already done, a collection, not a movement into the future.

I am at a new stage of life. I would like the pleasant-to-ecstatic feeling of excitement again, but I know that it must be accompanied by fear. Tired of fear, I am giving up excitement, too.

Is there another way? I am moving from excitement to enjoyment. An example: I started my beginner folk dance class last night. I enjoyed teaching it; but it didn't excite me. Will enjoyment be enough—or is there something I am missing in the discussion?

I hate to settle back into the position of "being a sage." Wise and measured is so boring. I want to take risks and dream high. But I need a dream to push me. The tour business was once such a dream; so were giving concerts, writing, winning great wealth in the stock market, and even the idea of starting a folk dance franchise. I aimed big. My wife said it was unrealistic. In retrospect, she was right. But who cares about realism or wants to look at things in retrospect? These unrealistic dreams drove me on, gave me goals, and lifted my spirits. So what if I crashed with them?

What can I replace fear with? The only dream I can think of now is sainthood. It qualifies as a dream, since it is certainly unrealistic. But I am not the saint type; I am an artist. Can they go together?

Golden Chain Versus Iron Chain

Last night our Tuesday folk dance group opened. What a success! A great night of dancing. My teaching was excellent, and I ran the evening beautifully.

This morning I woke up disturbed by my success; it disturbs me almost as much as failure.

I feel tied to my successful event. I become its prisoner, held in place by a golden chain. (After failure, I am held in place by an iron chain.) Iron or gold, I am a prisoner nevertheless. The prisoner of attachment has no fun.

It makes me sad to move beyond attachments, and bittersweet to dwell on last night's success. What a word, bittersweet—both miserable and wonderful at the same time, it so well describes the prison of opposites, the gold and iron.

Ramblings

Last week, I printed Folk Dancing Made Simple by Dr. Zoltan Fok-Dansz, having unearthed it from the depths of my drawers where it had been buried for years beneath piles of computer debris.

I'd begun to think about writing a folk dance book after one of our dancers said, "Why not write a 'Folk Dance Made Simple' book?" The idea would not leave my mind.

I designed and printed the title page on my computer. First I thought about making the text blank pages, but after running it by Ginger and Jim, I decided to use text.

I am printing and publishing my own work. I am planning to spend practically no money on it. I shall design all books on my own computer. "Books" may not even be a good description of them. They are more in the line of pamphlets, pages, giveaways, brochures, and fliers. Home-Grown Books: a good name for this "new publishing company." I'll have to learn more "publishing techniques" on my computers—like columns, graphics, lines, etc. My books and printings will be more personal.

This is the way my business is going, too: more personal. I'm in the process of giving up all my plans to develop a large tour company, many weekends, and franchised folk dancing. It was a nice dream while it lasted, but, due to lack of customer response, it died.

My new personal business idea is very hands-on. I can see, feel, touch, smell, and hear my folk dancers, my tour registrants, and weekend participants. They're either dancing right in front of my eyes, or they're a phone call away. I'll soon be cutting my mailing list back to the people I know or almost know. No more trying to bring all people into my realm. Why should I search for them anymore? Let them search for me.

I'm giving up on running my business. Let God run it. I'll work for Him. It's much easier that way. He knows what He's doing and where the business is. And He can bring in the business. I'd rather work for God, anyway. My job is simply to do the best I can, neither seek nor avoid: take what comes. God will do the rest. He'll even publish my books for me. I like that.

Beyond the Realm of Okay

I'm ready to work, try, strain and make an effort, to move, to roll and rise. I'm back. Folk dance classes are in order; tours, excluding

Bulgaria, are in order; weekends are in order. Work has started. Everything is in as good shape as it can be. My job now is to fill orders, be a clerk in my business, and serve my customers adequately.

Adequate is good; it is in the Realm of Okay. But what about stretchorama? What about the tinsel at the top of the ladder? I'll never find a whalebone if I simply swim in the Realm of Okay. Okay keeps you close to the shore. No question, you need it for adequate sailing. But to roam the desert, find trees in treeless plains, whales where there is no water, fish flying, swim in desert sand, to imagine, reach, and ignite the impossible—for that you must stretch beyond the okay. Time to drive down Hope and Promise road, visit my castle beyond the sun, and my dream beyond dynasty.

How can I do this? And where? First comes the Avenue of Time, second, the Avenue of Push. Time and Push are sandwiched in the city of High Hopes, where the No-Hope Sanitation Department (NHSD) sweeps the streets clean of ideas every morning. High Hopes is my city. I want to visit its streets and roam there once more.

I've taken a break to start up my folk dance classes, tours, and weekends. Now, after mucho expenses and psychological energy, Mother Business has returned to her den. All the children are back in school. "March! Get the hell out of here!" she says. "It's time for you twerps to be on your own." She points to the door with her warped and wizened finger. I fly out along with my brothers and sisters. Where will I go? Guitar Land? The City of Viking Literature? Writing-Behind-Doom? Latin Linguistics or the state of Yoga-Beyond-Yoni? The United States of Business is in order. I am ready to move on to higher ratings. How about the Land of Writing Copy?

Don't rule out sales and business.

That's the way I want to go. Grind up the old habits. Burn them up in the fire of hard work, selfless service, and push-beyond-limits.

Quantity will turn into quality time, breaking barriers and creating the Shine-That- Refreshes.

Folk Dance Mammal

The life of a mammal is sometimes too much for me. Ah, to be a worm again! My folk dancers met last night and again they peppered the floor with their dances. Feet spun webs of harmony as pulse-throbbing Balkan music salted the room. Our wooden dance floor spoke with the ancient insight of the old trees sawed into planks and laid beneath our feet. "Wood," cried Marge. She was from the English Country Dance Society. "Touch our feet with wonder; lace our minds to the higher cosmos where clouds grow on trees and leaves float across the skies.

"Oh roots, suck at the fortress of my soul. Suck up our essence. Spit it across our dance floor, then polish our souls for the final ascent." Marge inspired the rest. Soon our dancers were busy tearing up the floor and appropriating wooden "pieces of soul" for their private use.

When the whole floor had been destroyed but folk dancer passion was still not spent, many started pounding on the walls and ceiling, tearing them down and carting them off to waiting cars to share their heavenly loot with relatives and friends.

Our group is now being sued for damages. We must also find a new dance space.

Luckily, this morning the Church of the Holy Specters offered us their conference room for Tuesday nights. Our group was overjoyed, especially when they heard it had a delicious wooden floor! We'll start dancing there next week.

Marge's action was typical. Our folk dancers are a hardy bunch. They will not stop merely because an idea is insane. Most of them show up at my dance classes because they expect to find some ideas that are insane. They mainly hope to find them in me.

And it's true. I emanate insane ideas both verbally and through the soles of my shoes. My dance steps are secret cabalistic rituals, which, if used correctly, call up hidden forces from within.

This is what my dancers crave.

Many even want to travel and dance on distant planets. Their interest sparked the creation of my folk dance travel company. We plan to tour, not only the distant planets, but mind- sets beyond the stars as well.

Future tours include a voyage to the Protein Galaxy, north of the Milky Way, a visit to a Bulgarian amoeba factory and a week's retreat among the dancing protozoa of Romania.

Faith

Yesterday I had a breakdown of faith in myself and God. In the morning I sat at the edge of financial disaster; by evening I had received registrations from three new tour members, with the poss-ibility of registrations from two more. That's five people dropped into my lap. Who is sending them? God, of course.

There was no reason to lose faith. Yet I had. Losing faith is part of the testing process.

Suddenly, I returned to faith with a vengeance, furious at myself for backsliding. Sure enough, once I had, new tour registrants came in. Notice I didn't actually do anything. I only thought differently.

Business

After the Thanksgiving weekend fiasco, tour registrations started coming in. I tried to suppress my excitement. But on Sunday, when I got three more, I became overexcited.

Suppose my fear of business comes, not from rejection, but from overexcitement. Can excitement hurt as much as depression? It's easier to get a cold, sniffles, or sore throat than to face the frightening pos-sibilities of yoga stretches beyond my wildest imagination and floods of tour registration.

This could blow my business wide open. I could admit to loving it. Soon "sales" may become a word of power and beauty. Business certainly has the ability to pull many facets of my life together. I just have to shed some of its negative images. That could take twenty or thirty years. It seems like a lot of time for shedding. But my guitar breakthrough took almost twenty-five loving years.

Building Tours

We saw The Twelve Chairs last night. A lovely film. It reminded me of my first tour to the Soviet Union and Hungary. What adventures! These tours were highlights of my life. What suffering, too! I trembled in preparation for a whole year. But first births are most difficult; instead of trying to climb a new mountain, my future challenge is to climb even higher on the old one. The tour business is the most emotionally challenging and potentially profitable of my businesses, the place I can develop my language and organizational skills, test my knowledge of history, and make more money.

I could specialize in Eastern Europe with Turkey and Israel on the side. I could expand my tours to include France, Italy, Spain, Scandinavia, and the Baltic republics. Or I could take my folklore theme and build from there.

Limitations and Leadership: The Ten-Minute Rule

Last night's folk dancing was a misery. When Mindy taught the "Turkish" dance, it turned out to be only half Turkish: Turkish music with Israeli choreography. Immediately I saw Ginny and Hal leave the circle; a few others followed. Ginny and Hal hate Israeli dances.

When I took the chance of letting Mindy teach, I should have told her about the ten-minute rule. But I hadn't invented it yet. It is my new limitation for nonprofessional folk dance teachers. It gives them ten minutes to teach their dance. This cuts down my risk of boring and alienating my students.

Defining limitations is a blessing to the students, too. They define not only the borders of creativity but the borders of destruction as well.

Limitations can save you from insanity and humiliation. They have certainly saved me.

INVENTIONS

Theseus

Theseus grabbed Ariadne's thread and headed towards the labyrinth. Stars shone red that night, and the walls of distant turrets percolated under the hot, luminescent Cretan sun.

"It's much better underground," he cried. "Labyrinth walls protect me from sunstroke. But no walls can protect me from the paws of the Minotaur. If I can dance the syrtos, will his savage mind be soothed? I cannot be sure. I have never met this creature. He may like Egyptian dances or horas from the Getae of the not-yet Romania. Perhaps he isn't as bad as others make him out to be. Minotaurs have problems of their own. You can't tell what living in a labyrinth all your life will do to you.

Perhaps this one needs someone to talk to, a consciousness-raising group, maybe some peaches from Rhodes. I shouldn't prejudge him, even if he does have horns."

Theseus held Ariadne's thread as he danced syrtos into the labyrinth. Fours days later, he met the Minotaur at a bend in the tunnel. "I love hasapicos!" roared the Minotaur. "And you know something? I want to retire in Constantinople sometime in the next three thousand years."

Theseus and the Minotaur argued about hasapicos versus syrtos and the importance of dancing the Miserlou in Pittsburgh.

After two days of dance competition, Theseus finally shouted: "Hasapicos fans do not deserve to live!"

Then he piled syrtos upon hasapicos, slew the Minotaur, and threaded his way back to Ariadne.

Adam

In the beginning God created heaven, earth, the seas, sky, grass, and animals. Then He created Adam as a solo dancer.

But God soon tired of solos. "Partner dances are better," He said. "Let Adam have a partner." So He created Eve for couple dancing. Adam and Eve danced beautifully in their garden —first a waltz, then the Swedish Hambo. Although it is only implied in the bible, the later terpsichorean works of Blobbo the Elder, researcher for the Byblus Times from 1146 to 1105 B.C., suggest that all forms for today's folk dances were conceived by Adam and Eve.

Adam had a special fondness for future Bulgarian rhythms; he danced proto-ruchenitzas and pravos in his garden. He even invented the rhythm for the kopanitza when he used his hands to kopan (dig) up the earth in 11/16th time. Eve played the flute.

Dr. Kirby Bentworth, researcher and Chairperson of the Dichotomous Studies Department at Bladder-on-Tyme University, believes Adam's dance notations from the Garden of Eden were passed down from generation to generation to the present. That is why when we folk dance today we often say we're in paradise.

GOD

Thinking Differently

I played the guitar focusing on wrist and stomach.
One wrist. One stomach.
My fingers flew!
I have transcended the tyranny of notes and tone.

Yesterday I got four new registrations for Budapest and Prague. That brings my numbers up to twenty-two. I'm almost full! Can you imagine? My Greek tour has fifteen registrants already. This gives me more registrants than I have ever had in my life! And I've still got two and a half months to go for Budapest and Prague, and almost five for Greece. This is turning into my best year ever.

Why are all these good things happening to me? Am I doing or thinking something different? Is this happening through my own doing, or is God simply being nice to me?

Vivekananda says, "We are the God of the universe. In worshiping God we have always been worshiping our own hidden Self." If this is so, then I should look to an inner transformation.

www.ingramcontent.com/pod-product-compliance
Lightning Source LLC
Chambersburg PA
CBHW071421090426
42737CB00011B/1534